Faith And
Delusion

Faith And Delusion

THE SPIRITUAL HISTORY OF THE WORLD

An Overview from the Perspective of Orthodox Christian Apologetics

by Father Nikita Grigoriev

Order this book online at www.trafford.com
or email orders@trafford.com

Most Trafford titles are also available at major online book retailers.

Printed in the United States of America.

ISBN: 978-1-4269-6953-9 (sc)
ISBN: 978-1-4269-6954-6 (e)

Trafford rev.05/11/2011

 www.trafford.com

North America & International
toll-free: 1 888 232 4444 (USA & Canada)
phone: 250 383 6864 ♦ fax: 812 355 4082

TABLE OF CONTENTS

INTRODUCTION

"In that hour Jesus rejoiced in spirit, and said, I thank you, O Father, Lord of heaven and earth, that thou hast hid these things from the wise and prudent, and revealed them to little children: for so, O Father, it was pleasing in thine eyes". (Lk. 10 – 21)

Jesus said, "Verily I say unto you, Whosoever shall not receive the kingdom of God as a little child, he shall not enter therein". (Mk. 10-15)

Humanity has strayed far from the pure and simple teaching that Jesus Christ revealed to his apostles and that has been preserved intact in the Orthodox Church for almost two thousand years. It seems paradoxical that as more knowledge is acquired of the world, the knowledge of God and faith seems to dissipate. This is because real faith in God can only abide in a pure heart. Jesus said, "Blessed are the pure in heart, for they shall see God". (Mat 5:8).

This book examines from an historical perspective the battle of spiritual delusion and unbelief against real faith in God. The entire history of mankind can be viewed as basically Satan's war against God, for the human heart. The primary weapon of the father of lies is, naturally, falsehood, along with distortion and unbelief. In order to survive and be saved in this terrible war of falsehood, we must arm ourselves with an understanding of that simple and pure Truth revealed to us by Christ through His apostles.

In order to acquire that simple childlike faith in God, we must strive to purify our hearts from intellectual pride and all the other sinful passions that reside in it. Only then can we hope to have that pure faith in God that can move mountains and, most importantly, save our souls.

This knowledge and understanding of God's Truth, this pure apostolic and patristic faith, have almost disappeared from the face of the earth. But those who seek, *do* find and to those who knock it is always opened for God Himself told us: *"Blessed are those who hunger and thirst after Righteousness, for they shall be filled."* (Mat. 5:6).

CHAPTER ONE —
Faith

Faith in General

What exactly is faith? Faith is the power of the soul consisting of a synergetic blend of the intellect (reason), the heart (desire) and the will (driving force). This is the most fundamental manifestation of all the properties of the soul, originating, directing and completing all intentions and acts. Faith is completely natural and is an inherent property of all conscious beings. Without any faith whatsoever it is impossible to function even on a most elementary level. It manifests itself as a certain trust, sureness or confidence, expectation and even love.

But this is not yet faith in God. This faith is not spiritual but physical or material and is altogether appropriate and even necessary with regards primarily to oneself, to others, to ideas and even to objects. Without this natural faith in oneself, it would be impossible to even get up from a chair and walk across the room. Without such faith or trust in builders of bridges, for instance, we would be overcome by terror each time we had to cross the bridge. Without such a faith in a currency we would find it extremely difficult to use it. This faith does not have a moral element since it does not include the notion of absolute good and evil. Such a faith is appropriate to a setting where a certain confidence in suppositions exists based on prior experience and rational deduction.

But faith in God is a matter of a different order altogether.

1

Faith in God

God is spirit. And the spirit of God is the Spirit of Truth. This is the Holy Spirit, the third person of the indivisible Holy Trinity. This Truth is God's Truth and it is not relative, subjective or circumstantial but absolute, universal and eternal. This Truth is the foundation of reality.

Truth is that which is real.

A falsehood is something that is not real. A lie or a deceit is a conscious depiction of some thing or situation as being real which actually is not the case or does not exist in reality. In other words, a lie is that which is not.

Truth is that which *is*. God *is* Truth and His being is therefore *necessary*.

In fact, the existence of everything else and of the entire universe is contingent on God's being.

Christ God said that "I am the Truth" and the apostle John, the Theologian, taught that He is the source of all being.

Moses asked God what His name is, and God answered "I am He who *is*". God is the essence of being and the source of all being. He is the source of life and immortality. God brought all that exists into being out of non-being.

God is also the spirit of love and of compassion. But first He is the Spirit of Truth. Because without truth, there is neither true love nor true compassion. Love *must* be based on truth. If it's based on a lie or on deceit, it's not real.

Satan is called the father of lies, of deceit, of slander. He is the master of illusion and of all that is not. He hates reality and life itself and longs for non-being.

Satan's conflict is with God, the source of being and of truth. The battlefield is the human heart. The struggle is spiritual. It is between the spirit of truth and the spirit of lies in the heart of man.

Every person has been granted complete freedom to choose between truth and lies, between the Truth of God and the lies of Satan. A person *decides* what he or she is going to believe in this respect. It is this free choice that gives the decision a moral dimension. This is why when Christ commanded His Apostles to go and preach the Gospel to all creation, He added that those who do not believe will be condemned.

Faith in God is the foundation of spiritual life. It hinges most directly on the precept of good and evil and accordingly, it is of a *willful origin*. Genuine and true faith in God is the fundamental good from which all other good proceeds. Unbelief in God is the fundamental evil from which all other evil proceeds. Why is faith in God the foundation of all good? This is because it is based on a free good will and conjoins a person through Grace with the very Source of good, God Himself.

Animals are incapable of not believing in God or of not loving Him. They are incapable of not submitting to Him, and so they cannot have a spiritual life, because they do not possess a moral element within a free will. Their will is only partially free since it functions only in mundane situations and is mainly determined by circumstances.

The spiritual free will is completely free. It defines a person as a being created in the image of God. The choice is free: to believe in God and love Him with all one's being above all else (the First Commandment), to trust God completely and submit to Him with joy and trembling; or not to love Him, to oppose Him and even enviously desire that He not exist, and in His place see a human (specifically, oneself).

3

The Canaanite woman (Matt.15: 22-28; Mark 7: 25-30) is an example of exercising free will in choosing to become humble or be proud, to believe or not to believe. When Christ answered her *"for it is not meet to take the children's bread, and to cast it unto the dogs"* (Mark 7:27), many would have been offended, i.e., they could not have humbled themselves. In order to keep the faith it is indispensable to become humble, for humility is the passionless and realistic assessment of our personal situation before God and people, the sincere understanding of our total unworthiness.

Stubborn unbelief proceeds from an evil will, for it is based on the lie of pride and self-justification. Pride is a lie because it gives a proud person a false impression of his importance, righteousness and independence. Unbelief is a lie because it refutes Truth, God Himself; likewise, unbelief is evil for it rejects the source of all good - God Himself. Unbelief is the sand and quagmire on which mythology and every sort of false philosophy is built without the possibility of true knowledge and understanding merely fading like nightmarish specters into the eternity of darkness.

True faith in God is a spiritual light, brighter and more brilliant than any natural light, for it unites man with the source of light not made by human hands – God. Saints are people who are so filled with the Light of God that they themselves shine brighter than the sun and are depicted on icons with a halo, to symbolize this. Faith is the conductor which is necessary so that the power of God's Grace can descend upon man. True faith in God is that fundamental driving force unto which all the material powers and all laws of nature are in subjection. True faith in God is that rock on which true knowledge and understanding are built.

Finally, true faith in God is God's gift to a pure heart that sincerely desires it. This is God's gift to a good and free will that is ready to demonstrate courage and decisiveness in seeking Him and also God's gift to the mind which has humbled and bowed itself down sufficiently in order to enter through the extremely narrow gates into the Kingdom of Faith, into the joy of God, into the Heavenly Kingdom.

Man is created in such a way that his soul cannot live without true faith in God just as his body cannot live without breathing. This faith is unique for it can only be directed toward God alone. It should occupy the uppermost position in the heart of man. If this faith ceases to be directed toward God, then invariably it becomes directed at a replacement, at an idol. This is what is known as spiritual adultery and God is jealous ("I the Lord thy God am a jealous God" (Ex. 20:5)), He does not tolerate infidelity.

If this faith, which is intended only for the True God, is removed from God and not transferred to another, then such a man simply cannot function psychologically even on a daily, worldly level. Therefore, when this basic faith ceases to be directed toward God, it unavoidably is transferred to one of three things:

1. to created beings – this is idolatry; it practically does not exist any longer in its original form. This is the most simple, naïve divinization of creatures. Incidentally, real pagan savages easily receive the preaching of the Gospel even to this day as is seen, for instance, in the jungles of the Amazon or Columbia.

2. to Satan – this is Satanism; it is a rare phenomenon which currently is becoming increasingly more widespread. This is real possession by evil which is consciously opposite to faith in God and exists within complete awareness of God's existence and His commandments.

5

3. To man – this is humanism; it is the most widespread. This is a conscious but foolish opposition to God. This is an uprising against God and a refusal to submit to God. It is based on pride and falsehood. Because of having chosen falsehood, man's eyes and mind grow dull, permitting all ensuing falsehood to follow freely and almost unnoticed. This results in hypocrisy being accepted as righteousness and faults being viewed as virtue.

Humanism is based on pride and is the opposite of humility. This is the prideful refusal to have God in charge or to even depend on Him. This free and totally amoral and spiritually suicidal decision by man is the very central source of evil in man and in the world. Having made such a decision, man feels naked and very vulnerable. He senses fear and imagines God to be his foe, and therefore in fearing God as a foe rather than as the Father, he wishes to hide himself from God.

Therefore, because of pride and stubbornness, obstinately refusing to repent and become humble, man builds for himself a fortress of self-justification which he fortifies with pride as his mortar. There sits man in his fortress of self-justification and all efforts to show or prove to him the truth and facts become completely futile for the man has become spiritually blinded and will defend his own blindness with all his might.

However, God's Grace, like water, can erode away the fortress, and depending on its durability, the duration and degree of erosion, such a fortress may collapse completely since it is built on the sands of doubt and cemented with the mortar of pride. Even though the erosion may take a long time, the collapse often happens instantaneously.

This state is known as contrition of heart and is the beginning of genuine repentance. This is the utter vanquishing of pride, bringing one to stand humbly before God, sensing only one's nakedness and complete unworthiness, just as the Prodigal Son or Apostle Paul had done.

This is no longer a prideful and stubborn resistance against God, but solely a humble desire for forgiveness. This is the complete awareness of one's unworthiness to be received as a son, and a desire to at least be remembered in the Heavenly Kingdom, as the thief on the cross.

This contrition is accompanied by profuse tears, but tears of true repentance. These are special tears, the tears of true repentance, for there are many different kinds of tears and they differ even in their chemical composition. Tears of irritation to the eye are chemically different from tears that relieve emotional stress. Tears of contrition are tears that release many concentrated toxins that have built up in the body as a result of trauma or stress. A person can literally "wash" out some of the physical harm caused by the stress of a sinful life. Even from a physical standpoint it is healthy to cry over one's sins. But from a spiritual standpoint, tears of delusion, indignation or offense, for instance, have little in common with tears of repentance.

"A broken and a contrite heart, O God, thou wilt not despise." (Psalm 50). It is precisely such a heart that God will take and uplift, purify and adorn, array and joyfully lead it to His banquet and there quench its thirst. Christ said, "whosoever drinks the water I give him will never thirst again. Indeed, the water I give him will become in him a spring of water welling up to eternal life" (John 4:14).

CHAPTER TWO —
"In the beginning..." (Gen.1:1)

In the beginning God created the heavens and the earth; the entire spiritual world, both visible and invisible, all the laws, all energy, all matter, space and time. God created everything from nothing by His Word, according to His Holy Will. It was not by coercion or through some influence, but completely by His Will. God brought everything into existence from non-existence.

Having accomplished this, God will never return the earth and universe into non-existence. To suppose that God will return everything into non-existence is very incorrect and lies at the basis of an entire system of false thought which suggests that our world only exists conditionally and therefore, everything in the world, including all suffering, are of a mere illusory value. But this is not so at all, for God *"established the world and it will not be shaken"*

And God created all in six days *"and He rested on the seventh day from all His work which He had made"* (Gen. 2:2). *"And God saw everything that He had made, and, behold, it was very good."* (Gen.1:31).

Here it is absolutely and vitally important to understand that everything which God created in the beginning was *perfectly* good. Everything was indescribably magnificent and good without even the slightest hint of evil, harm, grief or insufficiency, and certainly not death. God created everything in brilliant perfection. In that primordial world there was no illness, no fear, no danger. The animals did not fear or devour one another for they were given grass for forage, and man was given grain and fruits. God created man for life, not for death. God did not create death and in the primordial world there was no death. Even fruits did not perish and upon falling from a tree immediately metabolized into fragrant earth. Not only was man not threatened by death or illness, but even fire did not burn him and water did not drown him; all the animals and nature recognized him as their king and master and served and submitted to him in love and harmony.

All that man had to do was to grow and develop spiritually. Man, created in the image of God faced an unimaginably joyous future, infinitely perfecting himself in his God-likeness.

CHAPTER THREE —
The image and likeness of God

From the outset it is important to understand the meaning of

    a) the image of God in man and

    b) the likeness of God in man.

Some consider that the image and likeness of God in man are revealed in the ability to love or to think or through creativity or some other manifestation. But all of this is only partially so and not the entire essence of the matter, for animals too are capable of love although not in the same way as humans. Regarding creativity, only God creates from nothing and completely originally, while man merely produces new combinations from previously existing components. But in general all of these are the manifestation of the activity of the human soul and exist only on an earthly level.

Pursuant to the mathematical concept of three dimensions one may draw the following analogy:

1. Physical existence can be considered as being one-dimensional or linear. It is the simplest, essentially animalistic form of being and is limited to a linear chain of causality according to the laws of physics. No morals and no ethics. Greater force prevails.

2. The realm of the soul is incomparably more complicated and vast so for the sake of comparison it might be categorized as two-dimensional, or like a surface, with

an infinite number of directions. It includes emotions, rational thought, creative and artistic endeavor; in a word, all the manifestations of the human soul by which the world lives. But yet it is limited by the plane of its life on earth, for everything in it is relative and does not embrace the notion of the absolute.

3. The third type of existence is spiritual. For the sake of comparison it may be categorized as a three-dimensional realm. Even though it initially connects with the realm of the soul and the physical dimension (since a person has both a soul and a body), but from that point it proceeds directly upwards. Although it transcends the dimension of soul and body, the basic concept is of movement up or down – towards God or away from God. In other words, the spiritual life of the soul occurs within the moral realm polarizing absolute good and absolute evil.

Movement within the spiritual realm is absolutely free and cannot be coerced. Although it can be strongly influenced by them, it is not totally dependent upon conditions of the soul or physical circumstances but only free will. But for upward movement, spiritual strength is required in order to overcome extreme gravitational pull and not return to the earthly plane of the soul's existence. From whence is this strength derived and how does one acquire it will be discussed later, but for now let us return to the human being created in the image and likeness of God.

The Image of God

God is a Spirit. The image of God in man is the spiritual image of God in man. Basically it consists of the person's ability to know good and evil and to choose between good or evil out of a completely free will (Gen. 3:22 "And the Lord God said: lo,

Adam has become as one of Us (i.e. One of the Holy Trinity), knowing good and evil"). The conscious decision to believe in God and to love Him means to freely choose good. The decision to *not* believe in God or to *not* love Him, means to freely choose evil. There is no power in the universe that could force a person against their will to choose faith or to refuse faith in God. The basis of the spiritual life lies in choosing faith in God and love for Him and, because of the inherent image of God in man and by the Grace of God, which man can acquire, man is capable of an infinite spiritual life.

But what does it mean to "love God"? This is, after all, the first and foremost commandment of God for man. It is important to note that man is not forced but *commanded* to love God. Clearly, man is left free to choose to *follow* that commandment or not.

God is not an abstract idea and God is not some*thing*. God is some*one*. When you start to love someone, you naturally want to know more and more about them. You think about them often, sometimes almost all the time. You want to be with them more and more. You want to share with them more and more. As love grows it becomes all consuming and you want to join them insofar as it is possible. This is what the term "marriage" actually signifies, that *two* become *one*.

This is the great and holy mystery of the Holy Trinity of God. Even though the Father and the Son and the Holy Spirit are three distinct persons of the Holy Trinity, their Love is so infinite and so perfect that it unites all three into One indivisible and inseparable God. God is One by virtue of the *infinite* and all-Holy Love that abides among the three Persons of the All-Holy Trinity. This mystery is so great and so deep that it is incomprehensible not only for the feeble and sinful mind of fallen man, who cannot comprehend neither infinity nor perfect love, but even for the clear and lofty minds of the Archangels.

Nonetheless Christ portrays His relationship to mankind as a marriage to which all are invited but only few choose to come.

Likeness to God

Likeness to God depends upon perfection in spiritual life, the degree to which man's spirit resembles God.

As already stated above, the *image* of God in man is in man's ability to know good and evil and in his free spiritual will to choose and to act on that choice.

Likeness to God develops through emulating God, or trying to follow His example by choosing good and rejecting evil. God is perfectly and absolutely good, and despite being completely free, He always only does good. Thus, according to the measure of growth in spiritual good and in the rejection of evil, the person is perfected spiritually and in closer approaching God he becomes increasingly God-like.

In order to help man along this path, God gave laws, commandments and finally Grace to help man fulfill the ultimate commandment which calls us to God-like perfection: to love God above all else with our whole heart, mind and our will and to love our neighbor as our self. Perfection in spiritual love is precisely that likeness unto God to which every person is called. If a person truly loves God with all their heart, all their mind and all their will, then that person will certainly try always to emulate God insofar as they can. They will strive to be as God is, because of their great love for God, not because of envy of Him.

Why did God Create the World and Man?

God created all that exists. God brought everything from non-existence into being through His Word (Christ is called the Word, or Logos, of God). It was not from some necessity, but from the abundance of His limitless love that God created everything in a perfect form in order to let all creation enjoy a blessed existence without need, without any sorrow and without death. For this lies within the nature of love – to share one's goods and desire that others may have the same joys as we. Thus, God created his final creature – man. It was with particular love and caring that God Himself fashioned man from the earth, according to His image and likeness and He breathed into man His own Holy Spirit, the beginning of spiritual life. And man became a special creature, the only one in the image and likeness of God.

Man was created as a spiritual being, living in communion with God. And simultaneously he was a bodily being, living in the material and animal world. Just as a sailboat exists on the verge of two elements: water and air; although the vessel is based on the water and moves over it, it receives its driving force from the air and is primarily intended for use in the sphere of air rather than under water. So it is with man; although he is based on earth and is sustained by material nature, he receives his driving force from the spiritual world and is intended by his Creator primarily for the spiritual life.

The spiritual life consists of the acquisition of the Holy Spirit and thereby the development of God-likeness in man through the growth of correct faith and love of God through the commandments of God.

Chapter Four —
The Meaning of the First Commandment to Adam

When God created Adam, who by nature was excellent and perfect but spiritually in an infantile state, He gave him one natural commandment for his spiritual growth: to not eat of the fruit from the tree of the knowledge of good and evil for if Adam would eat of that fruit he would surely die.

The question arises; why would God forbid man to eat of the fruit of knowledge of good and evil when man, created in the image of God, was precisely intended for this? This is because when man was in his primeval state he simply lacked spiritual maturity to know good from evil. Full knowledge of good and evil, while man was yet spiritually infantile, was not only harmful but even fatal. Why? This is because the knowledge of good and evil unavoidably entails moral responsibility. Given complete spiritual free will, spiritual growth and significant spiritual maturity are required in order to chose good and reject evil. Without sufficient spiritual maturity and growth, the responsibility which emerges from the awareness of good and evil is extremely heavy and unbearable for man. He stumbles and falls spiritually under this burden which exceeds his ability and this burden falls on him, choking him and eventually leading to spiritual death.

For this reason, in the beginning God forbade man to eat of the fruit from the tree of knowledge of good and evil. It was, of course, not because (as the devil blasphemed) that God did not wish that man's eyes would open and he would become like God, for that was the very reason man was created. It was, however, because God was protecting man whom He loved like a Father does, from premature and, therefore, fatal knowledge.

But man was tempted and fell.

It is indispensable to thoroughly understand how he was tempted and why he fell, for this has become the foundation of all human nature and has defined the entire course of human history which follows up until its last day.

CHAPTER FIVE

The Temptation and Fall of the Proto-human

The first fallen angel, Satan, watched man with enormous interest as the favorite creature of God, and because of hatred for God he plotted to destroy man. To this end, Satan decided to attempt to undermine man's faith in God and love for God, and by setting man against God he could gain control over him. Having studied man and knowing well and understanding God's commandment to man, Satan posed a well thought-out and terribly cunning question to Eve: *"Yea, hath God said, Ye shall not eat of every tree of the garden?"* (Gen. 3:1).

At this point man (woman) made the first mistake, by entering into conversation with Satan, who is full of nothing but lies and cunning. This cunning was revealed here primarily because Satan did not directly address Adam, but decided to affect him through his wife. Secondly, feigning innocent ignorance, Satan simultaneously blasphemed against God by suggesting to Eve that God had sharply and severely restricted them. And thirdly, he attempted to kindle self-love in man: suggesting sympathy for their very restricted and humiliated state, he thereby predisposed man toward arbitrary self rule.

Eve answered that God had said not to eat or touch only the fruit from the tree in the middle of the Garden of Paradise lest they die.

Then Satan immediately uttered a total lie: *"Ye shall not surely die"* (Gen. 3:4). And here then Satan revealed his entire hellish teaching, offering it to man in its complete format; a teaching which had been thoroughly thought-out and prepared especially for man; a teaching which is the same once and for all times for all people. This teaching is lethal poison for the spiritual life of man. *"And the serpent said unto the woman, Ye shall not surely die: For God doth know that in the day ye eat thereof, then your eyes shall be opened, and ye shall be as gods, knowing good and evil."* (Gen. 3:4,5)

That is all, yet **this** temptation contains literally all the evil which can afflict man and to which man is extremely susceptible, to which he succumbed then and continues to succumb until this day and will continue to succumb until the last day. It is essential to fully comprehend what is involved here.

Deification

It is completely natural that according to his heart, man wished to know good and evil and to be like God, since man was created for this purpose. Deification is the ultimate goal of man and the entire purpose of his existence. This is the indescribable lofty and joyous lot to which every human heart strives naturally and rightly whether consciously or unconsciously.

But the problem lies in how to achieve this desired goal of deification. There is only one path to this lofty goal and that is through Grace. This path lies only through true and correct faith in God and through complete, boundless love for God. Such faith and love, naturally, manifest themselves in a person's life in *acts* of faith and love, the main objective of which is to prepare the human soul and body for the receiving of the Holy Spirit of God, Who proceeds from the Father and is sent down through the Son to the One Holy Catholic and Apostolic Church of Christ. Then, man's deification is granted to man by God through Grace, that is freely, through the love and mercy of God and not because of merit.

False Deification – the Notion of Entitlement

But Satan offered a different path – his own. He offered no faith in God, but faith in Satan. The words *"ye shall not die"* meant that God was not telling you the truth. Don't believe Him, but believe *me*; I'm telling you the truth. God is not telling you the truth in order to artificially keep you in ignorance so that you might not learn that your natural inherent *right* is to be like God. Don't believe God's threats either through which he merely holds you in an oppressed and dark condition. Cast this yoke from yourselves and enter into your natural right to be like gods.

In other words, not through the cross on which one must crucify all one's passions so that the Spirit of God could rest within a man and deify him. No, on the contrary, the satanic path offers deification through unbelief in God and through brazenly seizing it as an inexorable right, and of course without any notion of the cross. This is precisely why, when Apostle Peter began to contradict Christ regarding the Cross which He faced, Christ said to him "get behind Me, Satan".

The Fall

And man was enticed by this temptation, and he fell. And man's eyes were opened and he realized that he was naked and was ashamed of his nakedness. Shame is the normal, healthy reaction of a spiritual organism to sin. Shame is a spiritual inflammation evoked by the conscience, like a spiritual immune system activated to fight and abolish the disease of sin. Shame flares up within a person, causing discomfort, even pain and demands the removal of the cause of the shame, i.e., sin. Having sinned against God by tasting of the forbidden fruit, Adam did not die immediately either spiritually or physically, but was instantly infected fatally by sin and *began* to spiritually die.

Yet God did not appear immediately to Adam in order to demand an accounting, but waited until evening in order to give the conscience and shame a chance to affect his soul and to make him amenable to repentance and forgiveness, thereby leading to salvation.

But Adam did not contemplate his misdeed and when he sensed God's presence he did not rush to Him with tears begging forgiveness. On the contrary, the first thing Adam did was to hide, demonstrating through this very action to what degree the poison of sin had already darkened his reason. For prior to the fall Adam knew well that it was impossible to hide from God. But, despite this, God did not directly beckon unto him and did not condemn him. On the contrary, God always protects man's free will and values it, and therefore deals very carefully and delicately with man so as not to violate the freedom of his will and not compel or force a man to submit to His Holy will. The more sensitive and receptive the human soul, the more subtly God deals with it, the more to develop it spiritually.

At this point God, according to His complete humility asks Adam the meek question: *"Where art thou?"* (Gen. 3:9). This question gave Adam a chance to come forward before God and repent. But even this time Adam, instead of repenting, chose the path of self-justification and said: *"I heard thy voice in the garden, and I was afraid"* (Gen.3:10). This was true because Adam, reproached by his conscience feared God because of his shame before God. But urged on by the audacity of self-justification and blinded by sin, Adam no longer saw a merciful Father in God, but a dreaded judge and he cunningly added: *"I was afraid, because I was naked; and I hid myself."* (Gen.3:10). Even though this demonstrates the childish simplicity of Adam's soul, but as well it shows the swiftly increasing self-justification, threatening to smother his soul forever and make it inaccessible to repentance.

It is almost impossible to imagine this great and terrible scene without burning tears. This is the uprising of a pitiful and despairing man against the merciful and meek God Who loves him boundlessly.

Yet again God endures the offense of this lie from Adam and asks him a more direct question: *"Who told thee that thou wast naked?"* (Gen.3:11). But Adam stubbornly remained silent. Then God resorted to the final and extreme measure. Since a more subtle and therefore potentially more fruitful approach was rejected by Adam, who had grown hardened by sin, God asked him directly: *"Hast thou eaten of the tree, whereof I commanded thee that thou shouldest not eat?"* (Gen. 3:11). Adam should have been completely overcome by shock at such a direct question from God, provided his conscience and shame still remained intact. But the process of spiritual death of which God had forewarned Adam was by then almost completed and in the petrified heart of Adam, only an embitterment against God emerged. And Adam responded not only with a reproachful self-justification, but even began to blame his wife and finally, in total madness laid the final blame on God Himself. Adam said, *"the woman whom thou gavest to be with me, she gave me of the tree, and I did eat."* (Gen.3:12).

Man, like a cornered animal, no longer seeing any way out, in despair lashes out against God Himself, Who all the while had only been stretching out His hand to him, attempting to save him. It was this terrible, tragic, but at the same time extremely tenderly moving picture, because of the boundless love of God which initiates all the proceeding interaction between God and man.

All of human history is a colossal history of love. The boundless and indescribable love of God for man. But on the part of man toward God, it is a history of predominantly and for the most part a gross ignorance, self-justification, animosity and disbelief.

But again, the boundless love of God and care for man did not permit God to deliver man over to that terrifying and unspeakably horrible demise which man prepared for himself: an eternal existence in a state of spiritual death, in other words, without God, without the possibility of repentance, under the authority of Satan in hell.

The Promise of Salvation

Having foreseen everything within the supremely wise council of the Most Holy Trinity, God decided to die for man in order to save Him, *"Greater love hath no man than this, that a man lay down his life for his friends."* (John 15:13). The death of the Son of God on the Cross, in God's providence was an indispensable means for annihilating the spiritual death of man and for his reunification with God.

Therefore when God revealed to man his future demise He also mentioned this forthcoming deliverance. God said to Satan: *"I will put enmity between thee and the woman, and between thy seed and her seed; it shall crush thy head, and thou shalt bruise his heel."* (Gen.3:15).

This seed of the woman is Christ Himself, the faith in Whom then, like a seed, dropped into the soul of Adam. Even though at the time his heart was still hardened from embitterment against God, but when the time came for its repentance, Adam watered his heart with abundant tears. And the seed of faith in Christ germinated and it sprouted roots into the fertile ground of the softened, penitent heart. And this seed grew into an enormous tree by which Adam and all his descendants live until the end of the ages.

The Banishment of Man – the Cursing of the Earth

Having risen up against God, man could no longer remain in Paradise; thus, for his salvation, God expelled him from Paradise. And God cursed the earth because of man, and all the laws of nature changed drastically. Nature and its laws changed significantly from how God had created them in the beginning. It is vital to understand this and to always keep this in mind in any study of nature. Through the fall of man and the subsequent cursing of nature, death made its first entry into the world, followed by tears, mistrust, illness, suffering and all types of sorrow. Animals changed drastically, fearing each other and particularly avoiding man. Man, who until recently had been the glorious master of nature began to be threatened by nature itself with danger at every step. Nature no longer recognized man as its king and began to entangle him with briers. Man was now forced to worry about his survival and exerting all his effort with great toil he could survive until he returned to the dust of the earth.

Death came into the world through man. Yet, only *spiritual* death is real death – an absolute and utter and eternal evil. Christ clearly differentiates between spiritual and physical death when He said to the man he called, to let the dead bury their dead, you follow Me. Physical death is temporary and frequently called "sleep" by Christ as in the case of the daughter of the synagogue chief and also in the case of Lazarus. Physical death is not an absolute and utter evil which is better forgotten or thought about as little as possible. This is God's punishment of man, as an unavoidable consequence of man's uprising against God, as well as an indispensable treatment for man's salvation.

The awareness of the inevitability and relative imminence of one's physical death is very beneficial for man. It brings him to his senses and provides the possibility of coming to repentance. The clear awareness of one's mortality proves to man that he is limited, temporal and dependent on God.

It is far more difficult to imagine that a man himself is like God (as he wished while in Paradise before the fall when he had not yet seen death ahead of him), if one knows that death is imminent. Remembrance of death sobers a man and puts all his life and all things pertaining to life and temporary existence into the proper perspective. Remembrance of death steers one away from sin and falling. Remembrance of death makes man avoid carelessness, shows him the brevity and value of time for repentance on which his entire eternity depends.

God placed this all before man, again because of His love and care for his salvation. Had man remained in Paradise having eaten of the tree of life, then he would have remained perpetually unrepentant before God and gradually would have transformed ad infinitum into a most pitiful, terrible monstrosity, exceeding even the demons themselves in vileness.

CHAPTER SIX
Limitations and the Chastisement of Man

God did not send man death immediately after his fall, but restricted his life initially to almost one thousand years. Nature ceased submitting to man, its laws switching from a willful origin, where they submitted to the will of man (as in the case of Christ and His Saints to this day e.g. The calming of the sea, etc.) to an autonomous regimen. Man began to feel like a stranger in a foreign land. All of this was sent by God to give rise to meekness in man in order that he might come to his senses and learn humility and come of his own accord to repentance, for where there is self-justification there is no possibility of receiving forgiveness. The absolute prerequisites for salvation are total contrition and a genuine repentance yielding the natural fruits of repentance: faith and love manifested in deeds.

Besides limiting man's longevity, his rule over nature and imposing a labor-oriented way of life, God gave man yet another restriction in the form of a woman for his edification. Along with sorrows in childbearing for the wife, God changed the position of the woman from a co-laborer of the husband to the position of his slave, saying to the wife: *"thy desire shall be to thy husband, and he shall rule over thee."* (Gen.3:16).

"And the Lord God said, Behold, the man is become as one of us, to know good and evil: and now, lest he put forth his hand, and take also of the tree of life, and eat, and live for ever;

Therefore the Lord God sent him forth from the garden of Eden, to till the ground from whence he was taken...and he placed at the east of the garden of Eden Cherubims, and a flaming sword ...to keep the way of the tree of life." (Gen.3:22-24).

So began the earthly sojourn of man and the history of mankind. This is the school where man, through submissive bearing of the lot apportioned to him by God, may learn humility and turn to God with repentance and attain salvation through Christ. This is the only way that man can be forgiven and be reinstated in the image and likeness of God, as the son of God through Grace. Now mankind faced the task of preparing spiritually to receive Christ the Saviour Whom God had promised him from the beginning, for the only hope would be through Christ the Saviour that man could return to that blessed state of eternal and joyous life for which he was created.

But the overwhelming majority of mankind forgot about the true, Orthodox faith in God and His Christ and, having squandered the faith through all types of idol worship, plunged headlong into dissipation. Evil multiplied on the earth in proportion to the increase of its population. All of the marvelous capabilities of their albeit fallen, yet magnificent nature, all their best talents and the entire one thousand year course of their earthly lives, primordial people applied not toward growth in God but to the development and perfection of evil and perversion.

"And God saw that the wickedness of man was great in the earth, and that every imagination of the thoughts of his heart was only evil continually." (Gen.6:5), for mixed marriages between believers (sons of God) with unbelievers (daughters

of mankind) quickly scattered mankind's faith having produced a population of spiritually vulgarized and perverted people.

No matter how glorious and developed the world's civilization was prior to the flood, all of it lay completely immersed in evil. Λ mere thread remained of the Orthodox faith in God and the expectation of His Christ, stretching uninterrupted from Adam and finally extending through only one righteous man and his family.

CHAPTER SEVEN

The First End of the World and a New Beginning

"And it repented the Lord that he had made man on the earth, and it grieved him at his heart." (Gen.6:6). And God decided to lay a beginning for a new world through this one righteous man, whose name was Noah, along with his family.

Almost everyone knows the story of the worldwide flood. How Noah, when he was about five hundred years old (middle-aged in those days), received directly from God, instructions to build the Ark – an enormous ship with very specific dimensions. This was by far the largest ship ever built on earth until the late nineteen hundreds. It turns out that the dimensions God specified for the Ark were the most ideal dimensions for stability and seaworthiness for an ocean-going cargo ship.

The flood was a unique phenomenon in the history of the world. It spread simultaneously and catastrophically over the entire earth and completely changed the whole nature of the world, from climate to man. It is believed that, prior to the flood, extremes were not characteristic to nature. It is presumed that in that period there were no high mountains or deep oceans; no scorching heat or bitter cold. There was neither snow nor ice; there was possibly not even rain, but only dew that emerged from the ground irrigating its surface.

It was much easier and healthier to live in such conditions than in those following the flood. The entire aging process was twelve times slower, and it can be presumed that there were significantly fewer illnesses since the human genetic pool was still young and undamaged. Mankind, being genetically fresher and not yet inundated with disorders, had a strong immune system and each person could live a normal lifespan of between 900 to 1,000 years in good health.

Some people find it difficult to believe that the flood waters could have covered the entire earth, as it is written in Genesis 7:19-20. They assume that it must have been a local flood, because they cannot visualize where could all that water have come from and then where did it all go.

Actually, this should not present an obstacle if one considers the fact that there is a sufficient volume of water in the oceans now to cover the entire earth to a depth of almost two miles, if the topography of the earth was all flat. Of course, the earth's surface is not all flat but now has some very high mountain ranges and some very deep ocean trenches. But there is good reason to believe that these mountain ranges were pushed up and ocean trenches were pushed down as a result of large movements of the tectonic plates during or soon after the flood. The top layers of Mt. Everest, for example, are composed of water-deposited, fossil bearing layers.

In psalm 104 King David , inspired by the Holy Spirit writes:

5   He set the earth on its foundations;
     it shall never be moved.

6   You covered it with the watery depths as with a garment;
     the waters stood above the mountains.

7   But at your rebuke the waters fled,
     at the sound of your thunder they took to flight;

8   they flowed over the mountains,
     they went down into the valleys,
     to the place you assigned for them.

9   You set a boundary they cannot cross;
     never again will they cover the earth.

It's absurd to say that the Colorado River, for instance, flowing slowly at about 4 miles per hour, has been diligently and uninterruptedly carving out the Grand Canyon during 5 or so million years though solid rock to a depth of one mile. That is simply quite unrealistic. Why haven't all the other great rivers of the world done at least as much?

Actually, water is capable of carving out the entire Grand Canyon in a mater of weeks, by a well-known process called "cavitation". Water can flow quickly under pressure, as was the case with the flood run-off from the high mesas and rising mountains. When the speed of the flow is sufficiently high, the pressure of the water drops below its own vapor pressure. This causes small bubbles to form and collapse very quickly and acts like powerful pneumatic hammer on the surface of the rock. This can pulverize granite at least as fast as large amounts of dynamite.

Quite clearly, God significantly changed the geography and topography of the earth after the flood and made a deep place for the waters to run off. There is, however, considerable controversy among scientists now regarding the actual physical mechanisms involved in the cataclysmic processes of the flood.Currently many interesting models are being developed which are attempting to establish the mechanism and sequence of events surrounding the flood and the earth's changes.

One such model is known as the "canopy theory". It suggests that before the flood there may have been a membrane of water surrounding the whole planet, either very high in the atmosphere or way out in space. The theory indicates the possibility that when rain initially began to fall on the earth's surface during the flood, the transparent water membrane surrounding the earth, protecting it from harmful ultraviolet and other solar rays while at the same time moderating extreme climactic temperatures (greenhouse effect) burst and collapsed. As a result, the globe was suddenly subjected to an almost outer-space degree of cold at the poles as a result of which the polar waters froze instantaneously. Some scientists apply this theory to explain the lush tropical vegetation on the poles before the flood, as well as discoveries such as a mammoth frozen under a kilometer-thick layer of ice in a completely fresh state with undigested vegetation not only in its stomach but even on its tongue.

Recent studies have placed this theory into doubt because calculations suggest that if the water membrane were more than, say, 5 or 6 feet thick, it would have caused the earth's surface temperature to be much too high. Most scientists have now abandoned the "Canopy Theory" as a result.

Another model being studied is called the "Hydro-plate" model. This model suggests the following hypothesis: when all the sources of subterranean waters on which land was formed opened up, the water jetted into the air under enormous pressure to an extreme height and returned to the earth's surface in the form of rain. The force of flow of this subterranean water contributed to the separation of the continents. Some scientists surmise that primordial earth was one giant continent which they call "Pangea", and that the entire surface of the earth cracked precisely at the current location of the Mid-Atlantic ridge. Through this crack subterranean water began to escape with unimaginable force causing in counteraction the separation of the continents, which slid swiftly along the subterranean water, propelled by reaction to the escaping water.

Because of the fast leakage through the growing crack, the source of subterranean water was quickly depleted. As a result of this, the sliding continents came to a sudden halt and the inertia of their movement buckled the earth heaping up mountain ridges stretching in long chain formations. In those places where the crust buckled downwards, instead of mountains, deep chasms formed which were filled with the flood-waters draining off the land's surface. In this manner some scientists explain the quite specific orientation of the majority of mountain ridges and gorges in the ocean floors.

The most popular flood models now base themselves on tectonic plate movements, which are believed to have caused numerous underwater volcanic eruptions and heaved up the mountain ranges as well as created the ocean basins and troughs. Although their movements are relatively very slow now, they may have undergone some high rates of motion at the time of the flood, which may have physically caused the cataclysmic events of the flood.

There is considerable credulity ascribed to the tectonic plate theories in view of the fact that they continue to 'float" on the earth's magma and continue to push against each other. This process is still causing mountains to continue to be pushed up and earthquakes to occur as the tension built up between slipping plates is suddenly released.

From a spiritual perspective, the actual physical processes of the flood are of little importance, compared to the spiritual process that caused the flood and the first end of the world at the time of Noah. Even though God promised never again to destroy the whole world with water, nonetheless, He did say that at the time of the Second Coming of Christ, the world will be comparable to the day Noah went into the Ark. Almost everyone in the world will be completely immersed in their daily worldly cares and completely indifferent to the fate that is just minutes away. The spiritual apathy of humanity will be just as in the day the flood suddenly began.

CHAPTER EIGHT —
A New Earth

After the flood God gradually shortened human life. First He shortened it by half; then again by half, and finally by yet another half. In the end, God had shortened human life overall by a factor of twelve, from 960 down to 80 years.

Now man was permitted for the first time to eat meat and drink wine. Furthermore, one may presume that human nature began to be increasingly susceptible to weakening and illnesses. This was permitted by God as well in order to bring man to his senses, for his voluntary repentance and salvation and was in no way intended for his detriment. God sent down all of this to man out of necessity, out of God's love for man and His care for the latter's salvation.

Noah's ark precisely prefigured the Church of Christ. It was open for all who wished to come to their senses, to repent and enter therein. But the world laughed it to scorn. Yet the ark was the pledge of future world, the ship which could transport survivors of a perishing world, the days of which were numbered, into a new world which was soon to begin.

This is exactly like the Church of Christ. And so, even in our days the similarity between the situation of the Church and the ark is not accidental. Today the approximate location of Noah's ark is known. But its witness is so powerful that the world cannot accept it, even though it knows about it fairly well. On the contrary, the world prefers to be skeptical with regard to it and once even attempted to destroy it, but God preserved and hid it. He preserved it through political circumstances in such a way that access to it is difficult to those who wish to treat it irreverently, abuse it or destroy it; likewise He hid it physically in such way that it is almost invisible to all but to those who conscientiously seek it. Exactly like His Church in our times.

Limiting Communications Through the Division of Tongues

Despite everything, unbelief and evil began to grow and spread quickly among people after the flood. People still spoke one language - that of Noah, the language of Adam. One can surmise that this was a superb and most sublime language. This initial language had been granted to man by God in a complete and perfect form. It had no shortcomings as we see today when we borrow words or expressions from other languages in order to convey a nuance of meaning more precisely. We can only suppose that this aboriginal language was beautiful, rich in content of meaning and extremely expressive, facilitating with ease the formation of ideas and precisely conveying the essence of any matter.

But the language of man is closely tied to the developmental level of his soul, mind and emotions. Because man fell and his mind and feelings dulled drastically, particularly after the moral degradation of the pre-flood period, his language was no longer anywhere close to the language of Adam, but it still remained the common language, a superb language inherited from Adam, i.e., it was close to being ideal.

Noah's descendants began to multiply quickly and inhabit the Earth. Noah's grandson established Babylon, that great capital of the new world. These were capable and energetic people who clearly understood that they could accomplish much through amicable, common co-operation.

But here, even given the successes and well-being, that basic evil which led to man's fall in Paradise began to develop rapidly. Again God warring pride surfaced. Again men's eyes were darkened and it seemed to them that there were no limits to human capabilities, given peaceful and friendly cooperation among all.

The people decided to build for themselves a city and erect a tower reaching to the heavens. They decided to do this in their own name and for their own glory, not in the name of or for the glory of God. This became a type of symbol of the endless possibilities of man and specifically his capability of creating a paradise on earth. But since they wished to create their own paradise by themselves without God's help, this again was evidence of the emergence of that same spirit of resistance and rebellion against God – the spirit of human pride.

And again, in order to protect people from themselves, from the unbelievably horrible consequences of their self-willed and godless efforts, God intervened from on high and divided the tongues. This was evidenced by a great miracle, a new order, a new law of nature. From that moment on people ceased speaking in the language of Adam. Suddenly a new nature of languages appeared. The basic original languages came into being and as a result, the various nations. Suddenly and for the first time there was mutual misunderstanding, bewilderment, mistrust toward other nationalities, alienation and division.

This division, of course, was not an original nor ideal state and it became a clear limitation for humanity. It became a necessary measure in order to halt, or at least retard the spread of evil on earth. Yet again, at the head of this evil stood the renunciation of God and the deification of man in place of God. This was the rebirth of humanism and the continuation of all the evil which naturally and unavoidably proceeds from it. Every nation, naturally, began to establish and define itself and uphold its own interests. Mankind appeared to fragment into cells among which boundaries impeded godless unification and, in general, the transfer and development of every sort of evil.

All these limitations – death, the reduction of lifespan, the division of tongues and mutual misunderstanding -- none of these is the normal state of man but a chastisement necessary to heal him. Therefore, naturally, a strong propensity for the ideal remained within man, a striving for the original state, that condition for which he had been created and intended. The inclination to godliness, immortality or at least to the extension of one's life and also to unification; all of this is natural and inherent to a normal perception of good.

However, the desire for endless life and world unification *without* God is absurd and insane, yet this is the very desire which remained in the hearts of those building the Tower of Babylon – the symbol of world-wide, godless union in the name of man. This humanistic wish concealed itself in the traditions and rituals of the Babylonian sages and this is the "secret" of the descendants of the Babylonian sages, that man himself is god and is capable by himself of creating a paradise for himself on earth. Not only can he create a paradise but he can create a god for himself according to *his own* image, likeness and even taste. This ancient wish had been passed down from generation to generation by inheritance, as the secret teaching for the "illuminated" members of many humanistic religions. Certain contemporary successors of this tradition, the builders of the new world order even identify themselves with the Babylonian stonemasons. But Christ told them well, first through a prophet and later personally Himself: *"the stone which the builders rejected, the same is become the head of the corner"* (Matt.22:42). That stone was Christ on Whom the Church was established like on a cornerstone.

But the builders of this world rejected Christ, preferring to use not the God-Man but the man-god as the cornerstone in their world building.

CHAPTER NINE —
A Special Nation is Singled Out

After the attempt to build the Tower of Babel, unbelief and superstition again continued to abound and become entrenched upon Earth. Unbelief in God became evident through idol-worship and the debauchery which resulted. But God had promised Noah that He would never again destroy the world through a flood, suspending a rainbow in the sky as a pledge thereof, something which was unprecedented in the pre-flood world because of its completely different atmosphere. Rather than destroy this entire unbelieving world and begin anew with one man, as had been in Noah's case, God permitted the world to pursue its desired path.

However, God chose for Himself one man, a righteous man, from whom He determined to originate a special, separate people that would be faithful to Him. God desired to raise and cultivate this nation like a garden amidst a wild field. God would enclose this nation from its surroundings and would perfect this garden until it would bear the fruits of faith of such a high quality that it would be pleasing for Christ the Saviour, Whom God had promised Adam back in Paradise, to enter into it and become incarnate.

The man, whom God chose to be the forefather of His people was called Abram. Having tested his faith, God gave him a new name, Abraham, which is to say, the Father of the Faithful. One should pause here and see the faith that Abraham demonstrated, earning him such an honor.

Abraham

Having chosen Abraham, God initially separated him from his relatives, sending him off to a new land which God had promised to give him and his descendants to possess forever. This is because of the inevitable factor of human psychology that results in there never being a prophet without honor, except among his own relatives. But prior to settling there, Abraham and his nephew Lot were forced to sojourn in the land of Egypt where they amassed great wealth.

It was pleasing in God's providence to return Abraham and Lot to the promised land with such great wealth that the land itself could not sustain such immense wealth, defined then to a great extent by the enormous size of their herds. So Lot took leave of Abraham and dwelled near the city of Sodom.

In the course of a battle with neighboring kings, the king of Sodom perished and his kingdom was enslaved. Lot too was taken captive along with all his goods. Here it was pleasing to God to reveal two events which, through His providence, entered into history serving to prefigure the Church of Christ.

"And when Abram heard that his brother was taken captive, he armed his trained servants, born in his own house, three hundred and eighteen and pursued them unto Dan.. and smote them...And he brought back all the goods, and also brought again his brother Lot, and his goods..." (Gen. 14:14-16) The Church regards this event as a pre-figurement of the First Ecumenical Council at which Emperor Constantine together with 318 Orthodox bishops clashed with the forces of evil, disbelief and heresy which were attempting to enslave a significant portion of the Church through Arianism.

The second event occurred during Abraham's return home after freeing Lot, when another King, Melchizedek, the priest of the Most High God, went out to meet him. Melchizedek brought forth bread and wine unto Abraham and *"he blessed him, and said, Blessed be Abram of the most high God, possessor of heaven and earth: and blessed be the most high God, which hath delivered thine enemies into thy hand."* (Gen. 14:19-20). In this prefigurement, Abraham is mystically portrayed as the progenitor of the Church of Christ by Which God defeated the forces of hell and granted Her the great mystery of the Body and Blood of Christ in the form of bread and wine.

Following this, God again promised the already aged but still childless Abraham that from him God would bring forth a nation, numberless as the stars of heaven. *"And he believed in the Lord; and He counted it to him for righteousness."* (Gen. 15:6). Here again there is an emphasis on faith in God being imputed unto Abraham for righteousness and virtue.

Thus, when Abraham had already reached the age of 100, his hitherto barren wife Sarah conceived and bore him the promised son, Isaac. Then what joy Abraham experienced not only because of almost a century of disappointment after which his beloved son was born, but also because his faith in God, Who had promised him this, was justified and rewarded.

But what horror and perturbation would replace his joy when soon afterwards God said to Abraham: *"Take now thy son, thine only son Isaac, whom thou lovest, and get thee into the land of Moriah; and offer him there for a burnt offering upon one of the mountains which I will tell thee of."* (Gen. 22:2).

Yet Abraham's faith remained unshaken. He arose calmly, took kindling wood and Isaac and led him to be slaughtered as a burnt offering to God. We cannot even imagine what was occurring within this great soul of the righteous Abraham during the three-day journey to the mountain. One can surmise that while Abraham journeyed in body for three days to the place of sacrifice, in his soul he remained in a dark chasm, prefiguring Christ's three days in the tomb.

And yet again, Abraham's faith remained unshaken. And when his son Isaac asked him: *"Behold the fire and the wood: but where is the lamb for a burnt offering?"* (Gen. 22:7), Abraham replied calmly and decisively: *"My son, God will provide himself a lamb for a burnt offering"* (Gen. 22:8), prophesying Christ.

Foreknowing Abraham's faith and in order to increase this wondrous faith to its maximum potential, God permits matters to proceed to the point that Abraham even lifts his knife over the tied Isaac. Having brought this scene to the final second, God demonstrates once and for all the wondrous height of Adam's faith as well as the meekness and humility of his son, Isaac. At that moment God sends them an angel who restrains Abraham's hand and shows him a ram caught in a thicket which God would accept as a sacrifice in place of Isaac.

In this manner God enables the development and manifestation of Abraham's faith. Abraham had achieved such love and loyalty toward God, that indeed he was ready to sacrifice his only and beloved son for God's sake, if this were pleasing to God.

But God did not need Isaac to be sacrificed; rather, He needed Abraham's heart. Therefore, subsequently, God Himself sent His Only and beloved Son as a sacrifice for Abraham and all his descendants.

And God entered into a covenant with Abraham, (or as one would now say, an agreement or contract was made), that the Lord would be the God of Abraham's descendants and they would be faithful to Him, recognizing no gods other than God Most High. And God would give them a law which they would be bound to observe and He would also grant them a promised land forever. And God promised to multiply them in the promised land.

Having apportioned His people unto Himself, God began the task of their upbringing. He gave them the Mosaic commandments, the prophets, priests, judges and later kings. Despite the fact that many among this hard-headed nation constantly succumbed to the temptation of apostatic teachings and idol worship (for which God sternly punished them), nonetheless a part of this nation grew spiritually and attained perfection, finally achieving the spiritual height of St. John the Baptist and the Most Holy Virgin Theotokos Herself. It was only then that the time arrived for the coming into the world and incarnation of the Son of God, the Second Hypostasis of the Most Holy Trinity, the Wisdom of God by Whom the entire visible and invisible world was created.

CHAPTER TEN

The Church of Christ

The edifying effects of the law and chastisement contributed to the salvation of the human race. God's chosen people, the Old Testament (Orthodox) Church attained the zenith of its spiritual height in the person of the Most Holy Virgin Mary. On this spiritual ground it was pleasing to God to bring forth the seed from the Woman which God had promised Adam in Paradise when He said to the serpent: *"her seed shall crush thy head, and thou shalt bruise his heel."* (Gen. 3:15).

Christ came into the world to reunite man with God. In fact "religion" in Latin means exactly that: reunification. In the Person of Christ, God Himself became man so that man could once again become god.

When Adam was created, he was the first human and thus he became the prototype, like a mold, for the entire human race. When Adam rebelled Against God, he fell spiritually and physically from that lofty primordial state he was created in – the very image and likeness of God. And along with Adam, all of his descendants, the entire human race also fell as a consequence, inheriting Adam's sin and the proclivity to rebel against God. *The prototype, or mold, was so severely damaged that God himself decided to come down to earth and make of Himself a new prototype, or mold, for the new man.*

Christ came to make a new prototype for mankind instead of the one that had fallen with Adam. In fact Christ is often called the new Adam because He became the progenitor of a new type of man, once again recreated in the spiritual image and likeness of God.

Christ came in order to save those who believe in Him from spiritual and eternal death by dying Himself on the Cross for our sins in order to redeem us from eternal death and hell. He died and then resurrected to resurrect His faithful followers together with Himself for eternal life of joy.

Christ ascended into the heavens in order to open up for mankind the path to heaven, to God. And then Christ sent down the Holy Spirit, Who proceeds from the Father (*through* the Son, NOT *from* the Son, as the heresy of *filioque* teaches) upon the Apostles in order to establish His One, Holy, Catholic and Apostolic Church in order to save believers through His Church.

The Church of Christ was created by the Holy Spirit through the Holy Apostles. The Church of Christ is the Kingdom of God upon the earth that provides believing and penitent people the possibility (for the first time after the fall of Adam) to again acquire the image of God through Baptism in the Church by water and the Holy Spirit. Having reacquired the image of God through Baptism, man enters that mystical Kingdom and again receives the opportunity (living spiritually by God's commandments) to develop his likeness to God through the acquisition of the Holy Spirit by which the Church breathes abundantly.

Conditions in the World during the First Coming of Christ

Besides the spiritual preparation of the faithful of Israel, simultaneously, according to God's Providence, two other unique conditions had ripened. From a completely material perspective, the Roman world was at its summit of development and stability. Its vast borders and superb infrastructure enabled the swift and successful spreading of Christ's preaching.

From the perspective of the human soul, the ancient, classical world had arrived at what may be called a "brilliant dead-end". This contemplative and well-developed philosophy had achieved such a height that it became clear that it could go no further on its own. Human thought had conscientiously reached its limit and the best philosophers of the day understood that for further development of thought, a revelation from on high was required.

All three of these circumstances merged by God's providence into one historical period, providing the ideal moment for the incarnation of God Himself and for the establishment of His Church, the Church of Christ. It was pleasing to God because of His love and patient caring for people, to wait until this very moment in history in order to provide the best opportunity for the greatest majority of mankind to recognize the Church and be saved in Her.

The Church is One

The Church is One. This is the first definition that the Church gave Herself in the Creed. One God, One Faith and One Church. In our current days for many people, this initial self-definition by the Church has become incomprehensible and even forgotten.

The Church is one, but it has two parts: on earth its counterpart is the church militant (because its members are struggling each with their own sins and passions, due to the fallen nature of man and in-bred tendency to sin), in heaven it is the church triumphant (because God has delivered, or saved those members, who were worthy, of their sins and iniquities). These two parts are integrally linked for they are in close communion and accord, as Christ said: *"and whatsoever thou shalt bind on earth shall be bound in heaven: and whatsoever thou shalt loose on earth shall be loosed in heaven."* (Matt. 16:19), (Matt. 19:18).

The Church is connected not only by love and unanimity of thought, but by such love that Her members become one whole body. This one whole body is the Body of Christ in which the Holy Spirit lives. This very cohesion is what Christ prayed for in His prayer as High Priest, where He likens it even to the Unity and Indivisibility of the Most Holy Trinity! Therefore all false teachings, heresies, distortions in teaching and schisms which violate the Holy Oneness of the Church place the instigators and participants of such things *outside* the Church.

The Church is Holy

The Church is Holy because the Holy Spirit lives in Her and animates Her. The Holy Spirit can manifest Himself wherever and whenever He pleases and is never restricted by anything. But the Church of Christ is the house of God and the Holy Spirit lives in the Church as in His Own home.

This is why the Church alone has been granted the power to bless and sanctify, i.e., to not only make its members holy but even sanctify the entire surrounding world and the numerous objects in it, ranging from icons to homes and even vehicles. The bishops of the Church are called *"sviatiteli"* (luminaries, edifiers in sanctity), while the priests are called "ministers of sacredness" *("sviaschennik" - Russian).*

God is Holy and His Church is Holy. Holiness is a power which causes hell to tremble and which the godless world cannot endure. This power and this light is poured forth abundantly by the Church onto each of its members who strive to acquire it. It is indispensable in order to acquire godliness, i.e., holiness, to which each of Her members, without exception, is called.

The Lifting of Restrictions

The Church is the reinstatement of fallen man. Just as all mankind fell in the person of Adam, likewise it rose up again in Christ. In the Church, the curse of God which man acquired in Paradise when he fell is lifted and in the Church those punishments and restrictions which God gradually placed on man in order to preserve and educate him are loosed.

But primarily it is death which is abolished in the Church. In the beginning Christ said to Adam that he would die a death; now He Himself says: *"Verily, verily, I say unto you, He that heareth my word, and believeth on him that sent me, hath everlasting life, and shall not come into condemnation; but is passed from death unto life."* (John 5:24). And Apostle Paul asks the rhetorical question: *"O death, where is thy sting?"* (1 Cor.15:55).

Immediately after the descent of the Holy Spirit on the Apostles and on the Most Holy Virgin Theotokos, they received the gift of tongues. This was a great miracle signifying that God had abolished the division of tongues which He had imposed in Babylon. Immediately prior to His Ascension, Christ announced to His Apostles, that along with other signs to the faithful they would *"speak with new tongues;"* (Mark 16:17). That new tongue may be the common language of the faithful which is spoken in Heaven. It is unlike any of the languages on earth, but namely a new, perfect language for a new, perfect world united by God in His Holy Church; a new language for a new man, resurrected in Christ.

The first sermon of Apostle Peter pronounced miraculously in a language which all the foreign Jews understood as their own, is a sign that the Kingdom of Heaven had opened up and that the unification of mankind was now blessed by God. The unification of all nations and peoples was blessed by the

Holy Spirit in the new Kingdom of God, that is in the Church of Christ.

Thus in the countries which had been baptized and entered into the Church of Christ, wars and internecine strife died down and peace and Christian love reigned. With the descent of the Holy Spirit the Kingdom of Heaven opened up and the New Testament commenced; a genuine New Age – the Age of the Triumph of Truth and Life over falsehood and death, the victory of freedom over slavery and Light over darkness.

Then all the powers of hell which had been put to shame launched an onslaught against the Church. At this point the history of the modern world begins, the history of the battle of Satan against Christ's Church. This is when authentic Christian Apologetics came into being.

CHAPTER ELEVEN —
Christian Apologetics

From Her very inception, the Church of Christ began to grow and strengthen quickly. Apostle Peter's first wondrous sermon brought 3,000 people, Jews who were from among those who just recently had cried "crucify Him, crucify Him" and who had laughed at Christ Who was dying in extreme suffering on the Cross. With every day new members joined the Church through repentance, baptism and the laying on of the apostles' hands in order that the Holy Spirit would descend upon the new members. The pagans did not pay them particular attention considering them to be some new Hebrew sect which did not affect them.

Yet the scribes, Sadducees and especially the Pharisees who were extremely enraged attempted to destroy the young, flourishing Church of Christ by any possible means. All attempts to physically annihilate the Apostles were unsuccessful. Threats against the people of excommunication from the synagogue did not affect everyone. The Church continued to grow and become stronger through the abundant manifestation of Grace and miracles of the Holy Spirit.

To the Jews

The first apologetics was directed at the Jews in order to explain and convince them that the Messiah, Whom they had been awaiting so anxiously and continue to intensely await, is not a king of this world, not a political leader who would conquer Rome for them. The Messiah is the meek and humble

Christ, the King of truth, love and mercy, Who is so clearly described in all their prophesies, particularly in the Book of Isaiah. He is the King, Whom they rejected and crucified, but God resurrected and gave Him a Name greater than any name, and all authority in Heaven and on earth, Whose Kingdom shall have no end.

But the majority of the Jewish nation, primarily among its leaders, the Pharisees, did not accept this preaching and continued to persistently grow more hostile toward the Church. It was then that Christ's prophesy regarding their city came to pass and it was destroyed. Their temple was destroyed to such an extent that literally there remained *"not one stone upon another"* (Mark 13:2) and the people were scattered throughout foreign lands.

The Jewish leaders stood at the gates to the Kingdom of Heaven – they would not enter themselves and prevented those who wished to enter from entering. God took His vineyard away from them and gave it to other workers who would bring Him the fruits of the vineyard in His due season. With this, the apologetics directed toward the Jews came to an end. For them, because their hearts were completely hardened in their love of the world, its power and its glory, the gospel of the crucified Christ was a stumbling block and not toward salvation.

To the Hellenes

Together with the rather unsuccessful apologetics to the Jews, the apologetics aimed at the Hellenes, the educated pagans, began to develop. Condratus is considered to be the first apologeticist, who in his letter to the Roman emperor defended the Church against the slander of the Jews. The leadership of the corrupt Jewish church, who personally could not manage to harm the Church of Christ God, began to resort to political means such as slander and influencing the authorities with the aim of prohibiting the Church and declaring Her illegal. This political manipulation from behind the scenes proved to be much more successful than direct public confrontation, and was greatly developed and refined over time.

However the pagans and Hellenes did not react adversely to the preaching about Christ because the Judaic resistance and hostility against Christ were not inherent to them. They did not stop up their ears in order to not hear the truth as the Pharisees had done during the Protomartyr Stephen's confessional preaching. In those days preaching was often accompanied by abundant miracles on account of which people easily converted to the faith. At the time a climate conducive to proselytism existed, for the preaching was fresh and inspired and one readily sensed the power of the Holy Spirit of God in it.

At the outset there was no need to precisely establish and define the dogmas of the Church, but as more educated and scholarly people began to convert and be baptized, ancient erudition and philosophy began to come in proportionately increased contact with the "new" teaching, Christianity. Therefore Christian truth began to establish and define itself in those forms and structures which were suitable for the purpose of teaching in academic institutions.

Outside the Church, a multitude of every possible variety of false interpretations of the Christian teaching appeared. Many false teachers began preaching differing variations of the gnostic teaching which was only partially Christian with an admixture of paganism and occultism. By the end of the first century of Christianity, already close to 400 such gnostic sects had formed. But of course, all of this was outside the Church and the Church strictly cautioned Her members to distance themselves from these sects and not be tempted by them.

Within the Church itself, two prominent schools of the time had emerged: the Eastern, originating in Alexandria and the Western centered in Carthage. The Alexandrian school had been established by the Holy Evangelist Mark and formulated by St. Clement. The Carthaginian school had been established by Tertulian, an educated pagan, who received baptism at a mature age and zealously undertook the teaching of the fundamentals of the Christian faith.

One of the main issues which polarized the eastern and western schools was the question of the interrelationship of knowledge and faith, or more precisely; what role does knowledge play in matters of the faith?

CHAPTER TWELVE

Knowledge and Faith

The division between knowledge and faith is not a natural condition for man. It had come about as a direct consequence of the sin and fall of the first man back in Paradise.

In the beginning when God created man, all the powers of man's soul were in perfect oneness. He possessed a masterful intellect, a clear and penetrating mind, a pure and strong faith with a holy and firm will. They all acted of one accord, in full co-operation and harmony.

When Satan suggested that man doubt the words of God by saying to Eve *"Ye shall not surely die: for God doth know..."* (Gen. 3:4,5), for the very first time doubt entered into the human soul like a wedge and split it as one would splinter a log. Since then, in the fallen, broken human soul, faith often became as if blind, emotional, irrational without the participation of reason, and powerless and unstable, without the participation of the will. The will itself weakened and grew wild without sound reasoning to control it, without the inspiration of faith. The mind itself grew dull, no longer enlightened by faith, and became scattered without the will's power.

The fallen human soul, in a state of extreme disorder, became incapable of functioning as it had been intended. Even the Holy Apostle Paul says concerning his own will: *"for what I would, that do I not; but what I hate, that do I."* (Rom.7:15). The fact that doubt shatters the soul, rendering it incapable of expedient activity is evident, for example, from the words of Christ: *"If ye have faith as a grain of mustard seed, ye shall say unto this mountain, remove hence to yonder place; and it shall remove; and nothing shall be impossible unto you."* (Matt. 17:20). Likewise, Christ said to Apostle Peter who was sinking in the water on which he attempted to walk and began to drown: *"O thou of little faith, wherefore didst thou doubt?"* (Matt. 14:31).

With regards to the fallen mind, the situation is no better. In the case of modern man, the majority of his mind is located in the so-called "subconscious" state, deeply immersed in an obscurity which is inaccessible for his conscious state. But now even in his conscious state man does not truly control his thoughts; he can barely hold onto a single thought long enough and clearly enough in order to follow it through to its conclusion.

All of this is the result of the shipwreck of human nature as a consequence of the fall. But in the Church of Christ Grace is abundantly provided for man and Grace heals a person, i.e., it makes that person *whole*. In ancient Church Slavonic, "to heal" means exactly "to make whole". Grace restores in the broken human soul the original unity and harmony for which man was created and in proportion to the increase and growth of the Grace of the Holy Spirit in a person, the divisions among the functions of the soul are abolished. Gradually man can acquire sufficient Grace to enable him to command not only a mountain, but all of nature in general and even spirits, without doubting in the least and receive all according to his words.

From an Orthodox view, there has never existed a conflict or rivalry between faith and knowledge. Both of these functions are understood to be different properties of the soul which are specific within the purpose of co-operation and unity in Grace. In the East, ancient Alexandria was famous for its scholarly achievements and the advanced level of its academic institutions. St. Clement, who founded the Alexandrian catechetical school, expressed his opinion on this matter as; knowledge which is obedient to faith, and faith bolstered by knowledge, mutually intermingled, comprise a beneficial accord between them.

But the western theological school in Carthage held a different view of this matter. It was headed by Tertulian who completely rejected the role of the mind in matters of the faith. He made a sharp distinction between knowledge and the faith and relegated the mind to an unnaturally low and useless position with regard to faith. Such an extreme position contributed to the development of the unstable western stance on this matter. This instability became evident later, when the faith of western man fell from its former height, while knowledge, on the other hand was elevated to an unnatural and likewise extreme height in comparison to the diminished position of faith.

But even this western partiality to a direct faith without any particular involvement of philosophy played a very important role during the era of the Ecumenical Councils, shielding the Church from being drawn into the confusion of many subtle, but often mistaken analyses proceeding from the inquisitive Greek mind.

CHAPTER THIRTEEN —
War Waged Against the Church by Satan

Physical Persecution

During the first three centuries of the existence of the Church of Christ, the enemy endeavored to simply exterminate the Church through physical means. The enemies of the Church slandered Her to the civil government, inventing all sorts of accusations against the Church upon which the authorities from time to time would launch dreadful persecutions against the Church. But direct persecution only strengthened and developed Her. The Church produced a vast assembly of martyrs who witnessed to their faith and devotion to Christ. They were inspired and strengthened by the Grace of the Holy Spirit and at times demonstrated such supernatural valor that all the bestial suffering and torture inflicted upon them by barbaric Rome proved completely incapable of turning them away from faith in Christ. On the contrary, the persecution of the Church only served to purify Her, making Her healthier, preventing the development within Her of an element of unbelief or weakness of faith.

Simultaneously, of course, gnosticism was developing, distorting Orthodox teaching, mixing Faith with every possible pagan teaching. But the Church remained as a separate, cohesive group, living by a pure, singular and strong faith, the Orthodox faith. The members of the Church were prepared, literally, at any moment to die for Christ. For this reason they frequently kept the Holy Mysteries (the Body and Blood of

Christ) readily on hand, so that if the need arose they could partake of the Mysteries right before the end of their earthly life.

But the Church triumphed over all the persecutions, and in the year 325, Emperor Constantine, having assembled all 318 bishops of the Church, proclaimed Christianity to be the officially recognized religion in the empire and therefore, beyond persecution. Throughout Christendom the building of churches and schools began, and for the Church a bright period of peace and well-being ensued.

The enemy of the Church, Satan, realized that not only did physical persecution not annihilate the Church, but on the contrary, the Church grew up and became strong on the blood of martyrs. Then the enemy changed his tactics and launched an intensive attack on the very teaching of the Church, Her dogmas.

The dogmas of the Church exist as one whole, organically connected, living body of teaching. This integrity and oneness of essence are derived from the Holy Spirit and this is why all of the Church's dogmas breathe by the Holy Spirit. Just as any living organism rejects foreign matter, like a disease, likewise the Church does not accept, but rejects extraneous teaching which is not of the Holy Spirit.

Nothing is more effective in disrupting an organism than penetrating into its very core and altering its DNA structure. This is why the Church takes even the minutest change to any of its dogmas of faith very seriously, like a spiritually fatal injury.

For most people the exact structure of a DNA molecule is not known nor understood, but they realize that it is exactly its precise and definite structure which is absolutely important, since it ensures the proper development and health of an organism over the course of its entire life.

It is exactly the same with regards to the dogmas of the Orthodox Faith, which was born of the Holy Spirit and lives only by the Holy Spirit, and the entire life of the Church, including morality and even daily life are a direct consequence of Her holy dogmas. Therefore it is imperative to understand, that any distortions of dogma, no matter how we might view them, and "insignificant" according to our ignorance, lead to profound spiritual injury and spiritual death. After spiritual death, moral degradation invariably follows.

The enemy understood this well and chose this aspect in order to destroy the Church, thereby depriving mankind of salvation. This time, rather than attempting to annihilate the faithful physically, he attempted to instill his own distorted "dogmas" into the teaching of the Church. When contamination by these false dogmas would reach dangerous, epidemic proportions, the Church would convene in Ecumenical Councils in order to identify and expel false teaching.

The Church never introduces any new teachings, for all of God's revelation to the Church was already given to Her in all its fullness by the Holy Spirit, from the very beginning of Her existence. But this teaching is assimilated by each person individually, according to the level of his own holiness and ability to contain it. This teaching is Divine, and as such, it is outside of time, and therefore, essentially, it never changes with time.

But the enemy of our salvation took advantage of the propensity of the Greek mind to analyze most subtle philosophical concepts in greatest detail. Arianism, Nestorianism and iconclasm were all false teachings through which he attempted to depose the Church of Christ throughout the four centuries which followed. But again, the Church triumphed through her seven Ecumenical Councils. The era of Christological heresies basically ended successfully with the triumph of Orthodoxy at the seventh Ecumenical Council.

But the enemy who had been put to shame did not cease his attack against the Church. He then devised a new and most dangerous temptation for the Church, which turned out to be, in a sense, the most successful for the enemy.

CHAPTER FOURTEEN —
Rome Falls Away

Rome had been a bulwark of solid Orthodoxy during the era of heresies and Ecumenical Councils. During the time when heresies sprang up and flared in the vibrant Byzantine theological environment, Rome, which was much more simple and tranquil often staunchly defended pure Orthodox teaching.

The stature of this ancient capital of the pre-Christian world had been diminished as a result of the relocation of the capital of Christendom from Rome to Constantinople. Furthermore, onslaughts from the barbarians in the west had ravaged Rome to such an extent that compared to splendid Byzantium, Rome had become a nearly abandoned city in a desolated West.

Almost all the books in Rome and the West, with few exceptions, were intentionally burned by the barbarians out of principle. As a result, in the West during the so-called "Dark Ages", there were not even any people capable of reading and writing. The only places in Europe where one could still find pockets of literacy, were the surviving monasteries, in which there still remained copies of the Holy Scriptures and people who could read and transcribe them manually. The simplicity of this situation as well as the inherent direct character of the Romans of those times, contributed to their stoic defense of the Orthodox faith and made them insusceptible to excessive philosophizing.

But the enemy of the Church, who had already suffered defeat many times in his war against the faith, now aimed his cunning at Orthodox Rome. The temptation which the enemy offered to the patriarch of the Roman Church, was very similar in essence to the temptation offered to Adam in Paradise. In Paradise it had been successful, and this time as well it turned out to be no less successful.

Again the enemy suggested to man that he become as God. But again, this would not be through humility, repentance, carrying of one's cross and through Grace, but through man's prideful insistence on his supposed entitlement. The enemy first instilled in the Roman Pope's mind the idea of his absolute primacy in the Church. He expanded this "right" to primacy to such an extent that henceforth all the other patriarchs, and thereby the entire Universal Church would be under direct subordination to him. This notion subsequently developed into the concept of the Pope of Rome being the personal "substitute" of Christ himself on earth. In this manner, the notion of the Pope's primacy was brought finally to its logical, absurd conclusion, "papal infallibility".

It became apparent that there was not a vast distance between insisting on the right of primacy and the notion of substituting God Himself on earth. Just as in Paradise, the human soul yielded to the temptation of having the "right" to be like God, likewise now man fell from his lofty Grace-filled position. And just as the personal fall of Adam would bring serious consequences for all future generations, similarly the prideful fall of the Roman Pope in 1054 would impact all his spiritual children and followers. Thus, not only Rome, but all the local Churches which followed it, fell away from the One, Holy, Catholic and Apostolic, in a word – the Orthodox Church.

CHAPTER FIFTEEN —
The Effects of Rome's Schism

When a branch is hewn from a tree, it does not die right away. As long as it still contains sap, it can continue to survive. Even the fruits on it can continue to ripen over a limited period of time until the sap is used up. But nevertheless, life in it will soon cease for the branch is cut off from its source of sap and life and is doomed to wither. While it is in the state of withering, externally it continues to appear as its former self, but it will no longer bear any new fruit and eventually will begin to deteriorate and rot.

This is what happens with any part of the Church, which breaks itself off from the living body of the universal Church of Christ. Such a severed group is no longer a part of the Church and no longer is connected to the source of Grace. Upon losing the Grace of the Holy Spirit, such a group soon begins to die spiritually and decompose morally.

Among the numerous and wondrous gifts of the Holy Spirit is the gift of discernment of spirits. If this gift is very important for every member of the Church, then it is absolutely essential for a bishop, and particularly a patriarch. Through this gift, the human spirit senses, as if by smell, any heresy, and avoids it like a putrid disease. When Grace departs, then spiritual sensitivity is lost and the spiritual eyes become completely blinded. In this state spiritual delusion is mistaken for holiness, and heresy is considered dogma. Moral decline and degradation follow rapidly ending in all forms of perversion and criminality.

Having been enticed by the temptation to be like God on earth, and desiring to supplant Christ God, the pope began to insist on what he had decided was his "right" to be the head of the entire Church on earth. He thereby violated the third dogma of the Church's self-definition, that of Conciliarity (*"sobornost'"*). The Church, in accordance to Her self-determination in Her Creed of Faith, is not only One and Holy, but also Catholic *(Conciliar)* and Apostolic.

Persisting in his error regarding his perceived "primacy", the Pope of Rome began to lose Grace, just as any member of the Church loses It through stubborn resistance against the Holy Spirit. When a person loses Grace, he becomes spiritually blind, and before long the pope agreed to accept a completely new dogma, the "filioque".

This teaching is pure heresy, invented earlier in Spain during the struggle against Arianism. In an attempt to emphasize the Divinity of Jesus Christ, these zealots concocted the idea that the Holy Spirit proceeds not only from God the Father, but "also from the Son". In Latin this phrase "also from the Son" is translated as "filioque".

This false teaching completely misconstrues the indescribable love and absolute, magnificent harmony among the three Hypostases of the Most Holy Trinity, One in essence and Indivisible. By very crude and ignorant means, it distorts the essence of God at the very root, to the point that this new god, defined through this new teaching on the Trinity, is no longer genuine, but another, strange, fabricated god.

Having added such a blasphemy against God Himself to the original sin of the prideful uprising against God, desiring to take the place of Christ God Himself, the Pope of Rome resembled fallen Adam. And like Adam, having lost Grace, he was banished from Paradise; similarly the Pope, having lost

Grace, left the Church enclosure and became, according to the words of Christ, like a heathen and publican.

Here it is very important to understand for an Orthodox perspective, that at the time the Church **did not become divided** into an Eastern and Western part. This concept is incorrect and false. People who split away from the Church cease completely to be a part of the Church. But the Church is always One, and always remains as such – One and Whole.

The West, which was laid waste by the pagans and estranged from Byzantium, did not have its own emperor, due to which the Pope of Rome gradually fortified his economic and political position to such a degree that he emerged in the role of the absolute master of Europe. His sovereignty was not limited to spiritual matters but extended to virtually all facets of life.

In the year 800, the Pope of Rome restored the Imperial Throne in Western Europe, occupied by Charles the Great. Charles, or Charlemagne as he is known to history, received the title "august" from Pope Leo III and became sovereign of the western part of the Roman Empire. But this was done without the knowledge or consent of Byzantium, and naturally, exacerbated the already strained relations between Constantinople and Rome. The instatement of a second emperor in the western part of the Roman Empire clearly contributed to the final separation of the West from Byzantium.

Although Charlemagne himself was illiterate, he was a successful warrior, and with the Pope's support he significantly secured his empire in the West. Imperial rule was advantageous to the Pope, for through it his own influence became firmly consolidated so that by the end of the first millennium it embraced all of Western Europe. Therefore, when the Pope split away from the Church in 1054, he drew away with him the entire kingdom which was under his subordination.

Partially due to the enormous scale of this schism, but mainly because of its spirit, this part which had fallen away from the Church did not immediately wither and exhaust itself. On the contrary, due to its scope and spirit, it became a completely new spiritual phenomenon, and it developed into its own uniquely horrifying and spiritually deformed entity with consequences for the entire future history of the world.

Chapter Sixteen —
The Fruits of the Schism

The Western Church had been completely orthodox for one thousand years. But the Pope of Rome preferred the power of this world rather than the Kingdom of Heaven which is not of this world. He split away from the Church, and from that moment on he became the head of a purely human institution, a false church. This false church continued externally to bear a close resemblance to the previous Church, but it lacked one thing – Grace. Grace is the spiritual power of God which vivifies the entire Body of the Church and bears fruit, just as electrical current running through a wire, or the vital sap in a tree.

Just as the presence of true Grace can be sensed, likewise its absence is also discernible. Having lost Grace, a person becomes blind spiritually and soon begins to lose faith itself. Upon losing faith in God, he begins to doubt the very existence of God. In this state, the person begins to feel that he seems to have lost the very ground under his feet, and immediately begins to drown, just as it happened with Apostle Peter when he began to doubt. At that point man begins in despair to seek something to latch on to, or in some cases begins to seek out a new ground for himself.

But there is only one Rock on which one can solidly build a spiritual house. By rejecting that Rock – Christ, man can no longer find Him through his own efforts, without Grace-endowed repentance. But a man is absolutely driven to find a foundation for himself on which he can build his world-view. Without a world-view (comprehension of life), man cannot live in a meaningful, feasible way.

Very soon after they fell away from the Church, western "theologians" began to invent logical, so-called "proofs" of the existence of God. The emergence of such proofs, basically served as proof not only of their loss of faith in God, but mainly of their *new* "faith". This new faith was ***the faith in the ability of their minds, with the help of logic, to grant them faith in God.***

Faith is a gift from God. If a man loses his faith or suffers from a shortage of faith, if a man wishes to obtain genuine faith in God, then he must turn to God, asking to receive it. An example of such a plea to God is the father of the possessed son who cried out to God with tears: *"I believe, O Lord, help thou mine unbelief!"* (Mark 9:24).

But rather than turning to God, the western theologians turned to their own intellect as the primary authority. This marked a radical change in western theology. Over the course of some fifty to sixty years, it had transformed to the point of being unrecognizable. Having been orthodox, generally speaking, throughout the first thousand years, suddenly, after splitting away from the Church in 1054, in only one generation, it had become completely humanistic.

CHAPTER SEVENTEEN —
Humanism

Humanism is a religion which teaches that man himself is a god and creates God for himself according to his own image and likeness, rather than the reverse. Having taken the place of God and having declared himself the proxy of Christ, the Pope became the head of the new church of humanism, rather than the Church of Christ.

In this new humanistic church, immediately its own brand of "theology" emerged, based on a certain profoundly-mistaken premise. This premise concerns a false understanding of the essence of the Wisdom of God. God created man according to His image and likeness and endowed man with a mind. But the difference between the fallen human mind and God's Holy mind is not only quantitative, but primarily qualitative.

The leading authority of this new western theology, Thomas Aquinas asserted that since God is *logos* (word), and man was created in the image and likeness of God, then man must also be *logos*. It follows that between God and man a certain natural mutual identity exists. Therefore, Aquinas taught, it is completely possible for man to know the essence of the Divinity by means of his own mind.

Before sorting out this colossal mistake, one must present the example of the teachings of yet another founder of Western humanistic theology, Anselm, Archbishop of Canterbury who by the end of the 11th century had stated that the man who seeks truth must direct his entire gaze only into his inner self, since true knowledge lies in God, and man can find God within himself.

Here one must note that this unbelievable identification of God with man, even to the point of essence, is an absolutely new phenomenon in "Christian" theology, and is closer in form to Hinduism. It reveals a total absence of any notion of God's *perfect* Holiness and man's sinfulness, particularly in his present, fallen state. **It is primarily this complete absence of any proper concept of Holiness and sinfulness, very characteristic of western outside-the-Church "Christianity", which makes its members prone to extreme and unbridled** *prelest'* **(spiritual delusion).**

When Adam lost Grace and was expelled from Paradise, he very quickly comprehended the scope of his indescribable loss, and sat at the closed gates of Paradise, weeping bitterly. With this repentance, his salvation began, along with the salvation of the entire human race. This is why the Church always begins every Great Lent with the remembrance of Adam's lament, for our salvation also begins with a complete repentance and lamentation over our sins.

But the Western theologians, having lost the Grace of God, having split away from the Church, demonstrated unbelievable ignorance and pride instead of repentance and lamentation. It was as though they completely forgot that when God created man according to His image and likeness, He breathed the Holy Spirit into the face of man, and man became a "living soul", i.e., he received a spiritual life. Such a Grace-filled state was completely natural for man. But when man fell, the Grace of the Holy Spirit departed from him and man lost his likeness to

God. After that, apart from rare exceptions, the Holy Spirit no longer dwelt in men, right up until the opening of the Church of Christ on earth.

When the Church of Christ was opened on earth, on the day of Holy Pentecost, people who repented could be baptized in Her by water and the Holy Spirit. It was through this means and *only through this means*, that the blessed state, when the Holy Spirit dwells in man, became again accessible to man. But the more a man sins, the more he loses this Grace of the Holy Spirit, and in the extreme case when a person completely leaves the Church, he almost totally loses all Grace. Those, who have not yet been baptized in the Orthodox Church, of course have not the Grace, and, subsequently no concept of the Holiness of God.

But the fallen, grace-devoid state is unnatural for man; it is freakish and a morally depraved condition, Man grieves deeply and grows weak from the emptiness and meaninglessness of life; but the main thing is that he himself does not know why his soul is so despondent. Endless distractions, entertainment, or indulgence in passions are completely unsatisfying and life resembles hell more than Paradise.

Therefore all attempts are futile in attempting to forget about the difference between the bright, joyful, spiritually alive, Grace-filled condition which is natural to man and in which man was originally created, and then the condition into which man fell and lies in to this day, a graceless and spiritually lifeless state. To speak of fallen man and forget about the fall; to speak of a man who is graceless and unspiritual as if that was the way he was created in the image and likeness of God... all of this is simply ignorant and ridiculous. It merely serves to expose complete spiritual blindness which occurs only as a result of a stubborn refusal to see.

To the greatest misfortune of the entire heterodox world, the mistakes committed because of this blindness formed the very foundation of Papal roman "theology" of the Middle Ages. And it was this same Papal roman theology of the Middle Ages which became the defining basis for the entire Western world-view, which in turn completely characterized the entire Western world, and ultimately spread and engulfed practically the entire world.

CHAPTER EIGHTEEN —
Scholasticism

Scholasticism was an attempt to rehash Divine Revelation through the use of logic. It is based on the faith in the ability of the human mind to penetrate and comprehend the essence of God and the creation of the world. The main founder of Scholasticism is considered to be Anselm, Archbishop of Canterbury, and its emergence is dated from the end of the 11th century, immediately after the falling away of the West from the Church of Christ.

The main objective of Scholasticism was to prove the existence of God through logic. For an Orthodox Christian it is important to understand, that such proof, in principle, is impossible for the following reason: faith in God has at is origin, an act of man's will. Faith in God pertains exclusively to the spiritual realm where the moral notions of good and evil prevail. Freedom of will, to believe or not believe in God is the basis of true faith. Only complete freedom of will, to believe or not believe in God imbues faith in God with a moral and spiritual value and endows man with the dignity as a being created in the image of God.

Any sort of proof, essentially, forces or compels. Therefore, a person who is forced to believe in God can no longer experience faith on his own, freely, from a pure and good heart. A coerced faith, just as forced love is void of moral value, and is essentially fruitless. Such a faith is in no way the faith which God anticipates from an individual for the sake of his own salvation, but is a completely different faith.

When Christ was dying upon the Cross, the Pharisees shouted to Him: *"If thou be the Son of God come down from the cross... and we will believe."* (Matt.27: 40,42). And indeed, they might have then believed. But Christ did not come down from the Cross, although He certainly could have. He did not come down because this was not the type of faith that He wanted and wants from people. Such a faith is not at all salvific for people, but detrimental.

Christ's coming down from the Cross would have astounded the Pharisees because of the omnipotence of Jesus and would have forced them to believe in Him. But such a faith is not based on repentance and is not voluntary. It is based on the rejection of the Cross and on the rejection of humility, and on the need to be captivated by the power of a spectacle, in a word, it is based on passion. This is why Christ said, *"A wicked and adulterous generation seeketh after a sign; and there shall no sign be given unto it, but the sign of the prophet Jonas."* (Matt. 16:4). A faith based not on a good, free will but on any type of coercion, be it either the influence of a spectacle, or out of obligation to logic is not a genuine faith and is not durable. It can never be satisfied and will always require ever increasing persuasion.

An enslaved faith has no spiritual value. Christ anticipates from man a voluntary, free and unfettered faith in Him as God and the Source of truth and all goodness. This is why such a voluntary faith is good in its essence and, in and of itself is the source of goodness in a person. Only such a faith is salvific for him.

Scholasticism was not a spiritual undertaking but a purely intellectual one. It attempted to explain Divine Revelation through Aristotle's system of logic. It attempted to adjust the boundless, Holy will of God to conform to the syllogisms of Aristotle's formal logic. Consequently, theology was reduced from its spiritual stature to the level of an intellectual dispute, where cunning argumentation and ability to dispute prevailed.

True theology is an attempt by the theologian to convey that which was revealed to him by the Holy Spirit in his prayerful interaction with God. This is an attempt to describe in words the height and depth of Holiness which are inexpressible in words. Theology is based on the personal experience of God's Holiness which has been attained by the fellowship with God of the theologian himself.

But when the West followed Pope Leo and separated from the Church, it lost its ability to commune with God, which comes only through the Grace of the Holy Spirit, the Comforter, Who abides in the Church. Very soon after that, a genuine understanding of God's Holiness was utterly lost in the West. Hence, Western theology, bereft of sanctity, became like the salt which has lost its savor, worthy of being cast out, according to the words of Christ. And so, it became subject to this casting out, for it had been dehydrated by scholasticism.

The entire fullness of God's revelation had been given by God to the Church of Christ from Her very beginning. Christ said to His disciples: *"Henceforth I call you not servants; for the servant knoweth not what his lord doeth: but I have called you friends; for all things that I have heard of my Father I have made known unto you."* (John 15:15). However, at that point, *before* the descent of the Holy Spirit upon them, the disciples *"could not bear"* (John 16:12), that is, properly understand and completely assimilate the teaching of Christ.

For this reason, prior to His very death, Christ promised them: *"But when the Comforter is come, whom I will send unto you from the Father, even the Spirit of truth, which proceedeth from the Father, he shall testify of me. And ye also shall bear witness, because ye have been with me from the beginning."* (John 15:26,27), that the Holy Spirit would teach them everything and remind them of all that He had spoken to them. And he commanded them all: *"tarry ye in the city of Jerusalem, until ye be endued with power from on high."* (Luke 24:49). When the Holy Spirit descended upon them and they were endued with power from on high, the Holy Spirit taught them everything and reminded them of everything. This EVERYTHING **is** the entire fullness of God's revelation to His Church, which is attained by every Orthodox Christian according to the measure of the purity of his heart and capacity to "bear" within himself this "incorruptible light of divine knowledge".

This incorruptible light of divine knowledge lives brightly by the Holy Spirit in the hearts of all faithful Orthodox Christians from the Apostles even unto this day. This is why Orthodox Christians throughout all the ages and everywhere lived and still live according to that one same faith, for the Truth of God's Revelation and the correct understanding of it is not achieved through human intellect with the aid of Aristotle's system of logic, but is acquired by the pure heart from the Holy Spirit. Beginning with the Apostles on the day of Pentecost and even up to this day, this Grace of the Holy Spirit was sent down *only* upon the Church. This is why that Grace is acquired *only* in the Church of Christ, in the One, Holy, Catholic and Apostolic, in a word, Orthodox Church.

Already as early as the second half of the 11th century, the scholastics were outside of the Church and, therefore, without Grace. Consequently, Divine Revelation and the Holy Scriptures became incomprehensible to them. When they rediscovered classical Aristotelian logic, they rejoiced greatly, for they believed that God had shown them mercy, sending them an instrument or tool with the aid of which they could finally understand the Revelation in Holy Scriptures, which up to that time, in their opinion, had been inaccessible to man.

They even believed then, as some people believe even to this day, that this had been God's purpose in creating Aristotle – in order to give mankind the opportunity to precisely and correctly understand the Revelation in Holy Scriptures.

Therefore in the mindset of Western theologians a surprising and strange, but completely consistent idea of a "developing theology" took root. The basis of the idea was that theological knowledge developed with time and accumulated with time within the common human consciousness, just like any other scientific or technical knowledge.

It is for this reason that Western theologians feel that, although the Apostles and the early Fathers of the Church had sufficient theological knowledge, nonetheless any contemporary seminarian knows and understands theology far better, since in his studies he has access to all previous knowledge as well as the entire accumulated experience of theologians over the past two thousand years.

Therefore, in order to resolve any theological issue, Western man turns to the very latest writings of contemporary (Western) theologians on that subject, the rationale being that obviously contemporary man would not resort to the classics in pursuit of answers in the field of, for instance, nuclear physics.

Thus, the main objective of the scholastics, although it was not formally expressed, was to prove to themselves the existence of God using their formal system of logic. This venture was based not so much on humility of heart and on a good intention to know God by any possible means, but more on a self-willed desire to effectively "acquire" faith in God for themselves, without repentance, without humility, but through sheer intellectual force.

This was an insolent desire to "acquire" even God Himself, without repentance, without love and without submission unto Him. Such a desire is extremely comparable to the desire of the fallen human heart to be itself like God, as well as by virtue of its supposed "natural" right, instead of adoption through Grace by God. And so, just as this insolent desire, at one time, had brought Adam to a subsequent fall and disordered condition, likewise Western society of the period following the schism from the Church, declined further, ending in spiritual disarray.

CHAPTER NINETEEN —
The Fruits of Scholasticism

Although the spiritual essence of Scholasticism was a humanistic endeavor, ostensibly enabling man to "overcome" God Himself by sheer logic, it officially manifested itself in three instances, or three "great themes", as they were called.

The first question or "problem", as it is termed in philosophy, was *ontological* and concerned creation in general. The concept that God had created the world out of nothing (creatio ex nihilo) was viewed as problematic due to the influence of classical (ancient Greek and pagan) philosophy where this concept was non-existent; furthermore by implementing the tools of Aristotelian logic, the result was that the concept of "existence" did not equally apply to the Creator and His creation. In other words, God's existence was autonomous (necessary), hence, it was completely independent and unconditional, while the existence of the world, including man, was obviously dependent on the Creator, and, therefore, conditional (contingent).

Such a concept, of course, did not tie in very well with the proud idea of man, that it was his right to be like God. Consequently, over the course of the scholastic process, such a notion was overturned. By the 14th century and especially in the 15th century, under the influence of the Nominalists, the notion began to prevail that, even though God had created the world in the beginning, *since then* the world had become self-sufficient and had no need for constant support by the Creator, nor for His care-taking. This was the premise for a doctrine which is called "Deism", which later became very widespread in the 18th century, after a "scientific" foundation was formulated for it.

This growing "independence" of creation, i.e., man, vis a vis His Creator, contributed to the increase of man's estrangement and alienation from God. Incidentally, all three of these "great themes" which were developing parallel to one another, achieved the same result in the 15th century, that is the estrangement and alienation of man from God.

The Scholastics' second question, or problem was *epistomological* and concerned the mind, or *"logos"*. It essentially postulated that since God Himself is *logos*, and since God had created man in His image and likeness, it follows that man is also *logos*. This is an example of a syllogism of Aristotelian logic: premise *a*, variable *b*, and the deductive conclusion being *c*.

But in the 15th century, the Nominalists took even this concept to the next level, reasoning that since God is omnipotent, absolutely free and arbitrary (of free will), therefore, they asserted, if God desired that two plus two should equal five, it would be so. And if God desired that any sin, for example murder, should be a virtue, it would be so. The resulting logic was that if God is indeed *logos*, His *logos*, however, is so inaccessible to man with his logos, that the human mind has nothing at all in common with the Divine Mind.

Here again, under the influence of the Nominalists, by the end of Scholasticism, man ended up estranged and alienated from God. And the human mind became completely inadaptable to God and to theology, yet it became very adaptable to created matter, of which man is himself a part, and to the study of nature, particularly Man himself.

The third and very important pursuit of Scholasticism was the question of *"universals"*. Here again, just as in the two preceding instances, the Scholastic process began with a traditional position, but ended up the opposite.

In the 11th century, at the beginning of the Scholastic process, a widespread concept prevailed regarding common species and types (genera). This concept correlated with the Biblical account of the creation of various species, each of its own kind. People believed and understood that common species, or the *"universal"* concepts, such as "a tree", "a human", "a star", etc., are of an *objective reality*. In other words, despite the existence of their individual, concrete specimens, in reality there exists the *"universal"* (*conceptual archetype*) of a tree, a human, a star, each having an *objective reality*. In other words, these categories and forms exist independent of our intellect or knowledge of them, and we do not invent these categories and forms, but merely discover them.

For example, when God said, *"Let us make man"* (Gen.1:24), at that moment the *"universal"* or general concept of "a man" began to exist, even prior to the actual creation of the prototype of man, that is Adam. Such an idea supported the notion of a Creator, since the existence of any *"universal"*, for instance *"man"* , **prior to** the existence of the first man clearly indicates that there absolutely must have existed a mind, *not a human* mind, which would have contained the concept of "a man" prior to his creation.

This position was called "realism" and corresponded not only to the Biblical teaching on creation, but even to Platonic theories. Although in his work, Plato could not avail himself of Divine Revelation, he might have become acquainted with it through the Hebrews; nonetheless through his amazingly penetrating intellect, he would arrive at the idea of a "duality" in nature. In this thinking, Plato almost touched upon the notion of the fall when he taught about a certain "perfect" specimen of all existing things. According to Plato, these perfect specimens exist in an "ideal" world, and are embodied in a far less perfect form in this imperfect world.

But by the 11th century, the new, radical and incredible idea of *"nominalism"* appeared, attributed to its founder, Roscelin de Compiegne. Nominalism asserted that general species, forms and categories **do not** have a real existence, as the realists maintained. In other words, the existence of these universals is not at all objective, but purely subjective, not existing in actual fact, but only according to us, in our intellectual structures and discourses. "Universalia post rem", i.e., generalization after the thing, was the argument made by the nominalists. Words, for instance, "man", or "tree", for the nominalists were merely a rending of air without any objective, real meaning.

Such an approach invariably led to "reductionism", the idea that everything, not only common, but also complex objects consist of simple elements. This means that everything can be reduced, or simplified into elementary components. All the forces of nature, for example, wind, lightning or sea tides, as well as any material thing such as a rock, a tree, a cloud or even man are comprised of simple forces or particles which are basic and cannot be further subdivided.

At first glance, for contemporary man, such a statement appears to be clear, natural and even superfluous. But in essence, it completely overturned all of mankind's world view which had existed up until that time. Without exaggerating in the least, one may state that the seed planted through nominalism, was the seed of the complete refutation of God as the Creator. This was clearly total godlessness.

The problem is that by ascribing ontological priority to the element, i.e., in giving primary significance of being or existence to the elementary components of anything, one thereby comparatively devaluates the whole object which they comprise. The more complex or structured forms of creation were tainted with the suggestion of arbitrary whim and inferiority. In this manner, all creation in general, and each of its separate parts, to a large degree lost its purposeful correlation (teleologicaly unique value). People began to view the world not as a majestic, purposefully correlated whole, but more like a box of building blocks from which one could build anything one wished. Furthermore, one could arbitrarily build either one object, or another using those very same blocks.

Overall, one may summarize the fruits of four centuries of Scholastic disputes with the following results: The Ontological disputes over creation ended in Deism, where man without God became an orphan. The Epistomological disputes over the mind also left man completely alone without the ability to communicate with God. And finally, Nominalism and Reductionism which followed, devaluated and rendered the resulting lonely universe void of any meaning.

Western man sensed that he was left alone, as if forgotten by God, in an abandoned and meaningless world. Man had already experienced such a bitter condition, void of Grace, when he was banished from Paradise, but at that time he had come to his senses, repented and began to live in the hope and expectation of his salvation from God. But this time... This time, the fall which had begun in the middle of the 11th century continued, when a large part of mankind fell away from the Church, and being left without Grace, they lost their true faith in God. Having lost the true faith, they did not repent in order to receive it back from God, the Only Source of Knowledge of God and True Faith in Him. They preferred to rely on their own intellects alone in order to "affix" God in their faith, which would not be given to them by God, but by themselves through the power of intellect.

But God eluded them and 15th century Western man sensed that he was alone. But this time, man did not weep and grieve as Adam had; now man had other plans.

Let us recall how all of this started in the middle of the 11th century. Was not the original motive that man desired to stand in God's place and replace Christ? They reasoned, that if God is no longer here and we have no means of contacting Him, yet before us lie limitless possibilities to learn and create in **this** world, then man will simply have to take God's place and assume this difficult responsibility.

CHAPTER TWENTY —
The Reformation

Any type of dogmatic wanderings into error, but primarily false spirituality, i.e., prelest - a graceless, delusional spiritual state, invariably produce the morally decayed fruits of degeneration.

The Roman papacy, which even then had been developing for five hundred years on the basis of its own form of *prelest* yielded an overabundance of obvious immorality, as was to be expected. Although some people understood that the matter needed to be corrected, unfortunately they did not understand that it was imperative to return to the bosom of the genuine Church of Christ — the Orthodox Church. They took it upon themselves to correct the mistakes and deviations within the Roman papal church. The Roman church did not react favorably to such reformers and burned as many as was possible at the stake. However, one of them by the name of Luther, as is known, survived and founded a new "protestant" church.

But again, this was not so much a new church as a natural progression of the papal line, that is *humanism.* Just as the Pope of Rome had not wished to submit to the One, Holy, Catholic and Apostolic Church, and wanted to become the head of his own church, literally instead of Christ, likewise, in this case, according to the pope's example, Luther also decided to become head of *his own* church, again ignoring the authority of the Orthodox Church of Christ and the Holy Spirit dwelling in Her.

It became so fashionable to follow Luther's example of founding and heading one's own church, that not only did the King of England, Henry VIII join in, but anyone who had such a desire, including even illiterate peasants. Throughout Europe a multitude of every possible and even impossible "churches" appeared like mushrooms after an abundant rainfall, each claiming to have the right to interpret Holy Scriptures and "save" its constituents.

The enemy of mankind was probably surprised to see the extent of his success and began to pour oil into the growing flame of delusional zeal which was scorching almost all of Europe in the 16th century. Vicious wars and battles erupted involving so-called "Christians" who brutally annihilated each other, supposedly in the name of Christ. Meanwhile, many of them were living a life of horrifying perversion themselves. Fortunately, not long before this, America had been discovered for anyone who wished and could afford to get there.

Many, seeking religious freedom of expression set out for America and began to settle its north-eastern region, New England, in entire colonies. These immigrants entered history under the general name of "pilgrims", that is religious travelers. Their colonies were called and to this day are designated according to their various anabaptist denominations. Some were called "Shakers", which means those who shake, "Quakers" which means those who quake, etc.. They interpreted this "shaking" and "quaking" as a clear sign of the descent of the Holy Spirit causing a person to fall to the ground, his body convulsing as though it were experiencing a seizure.

From the time of the Apostles, such manifestations of a "spirit" in convulsions and spasms were normally healed by fasting and prayer as well as through a person of sacerdotal stature capable of exorcising spirits. But these colonial zealots no longer had even the slightest understanding of either Grace or the true Church of Christ. Furthermore, in the Church, sin is condemned, while outside the Church it is justified. Sin can not coexist in harmony with the Holy Spirit, for the Holy Spirit rebukes sin.

Yet each local settlement of these "pilgrims" claimed the full and indisputable right to interpret the Holy Scriptures as each saw fit. Every member fully acknowledged and respected the same right not just among members of his own sect, but among all people of any other faith. Given such a favorable climate for spiritual liberty and human ingenuity, increasingly more new an even stranger cults began to emerge, approaching many thousands in number.

This concept became fundamental in the further development of American society not simply as a tolerance of faith, but essentially as the *equality* of all religions. The notion of the basic equality of all religions naturally conditioned society for the future development of the idea of "ecumenism", which only began to emerge two centuries later.

CHAPTER TWENTY ONE —
The Orthodox East

During the Reformation in Western Europe, in the Orthodox East certain events also occurred which were to have significant consequences for the future spiritual history of the world.

Byzantium had not suffered the same degree of devastation from the onslaughts of barbarians as had Rome and Western Europe. Consequently, Byzantium did not undergo either cultural or economic collapse, nor a period of "dark ages". It survived for more than one thousand years, if not without political intrigue, but at least in the true Orthodox faith with a magnificent culture. The sciences, culture, economy and technology were at high levels of achievement and Byzantium always turned to God's help to resolve its difficulties.

The strategic location of Constantinople contributed greatly to its influence in matters of international trade and to the prosperity of its citizens. But it also made Byzantium susceptible to attacks from not only eastern, Muslim countries, but also Russian, still pagan (pre-baptism) tribes. Yet God did not abandon His people, and always delivered Byzantium from the hands of its enemies, often in miraculous ways.

However, in the middle of the 15th century when the Turks threatened Constantinople, the Byzantine government turned not to God for help, but to the Roman Pope, who had a significant military force at his disposal. The Pope took advantage of this situation, and when a delegation of Byzantine bishops arrived to meet with him, he very skillfully persuaded them to agree with papal primacy and to submit to him. This had been an age-old papal desire and goal since 1054, after the separation from the Church.

Only one among the Byzantine bishops, the Luminary St. Mark of Ephesus would not sign the pope's demand. Because of this, the pope's entire plan collapsed, because in order for a complete capitulation before the pope to have occurred, the unanimous recognition of his primacy among *all* the bishops present was required.

Not having entreated God's help and not having received the pope's, in 1453 Constantinople fell to the Turks and hence the brilliant Byzantine era came to a close.

Russia, which by them had matured spiritually and strengthened its statehood after the Tatar yoke, received autocephaly and its own Russian Patriarchate from the Ecumenical Patriarch of Byzantium. This is an extremely significant event in Russian history because this 136th year after the fall of Byzantium coincided with Russia's emergence as a world state with virtually unlimited possibilities for growth and expansion.

The emergence of a Russian patriarchate and the creation of a Russian empire against the backdrop of all these world events is viewed by many as a Divine ruling to transfer the role of the main patron and defender of the Orthodox Church from Byzantium to Russia. These preceding suppositions are inferred when Moscow is identified with the notion of a third Rome.

Chapter Twenty Two —
The "Calendar Question"

After 500 years of relatively slow and smooth flow, in the beginning of the 16th century, the history of the West began to radically accelerate. Just like a deep river with an apparently calm surface concealing a multitude of currents, history began to increase its flow along an increasingly steep slope, to spill out across a broader and more rocky bottom, churning, foaming, breaking into a spray, rushing headlong toward the waterfall – into the abyss.

On the backdrop of all the events of the 15th and 16th centuries when Byzantium collapsed, when the Orthodox Russian empire was developing and growing stronger while Western Europe was undergoing reformation, it is important to not overlook yet another phenomenon of extremely important consequence.

The Pope of Rome, Gregory XIII, having arrived at the conviction that the Julian solar calendar in use then was not exact and therefore in need of correction, decided to correct the calendar with the aid of his two Vatican astrologers. Using a narrow ray of sunlight shining on the floor of the "calendar chamber" in the Vatican, they persuaded the Pope that the actual length of the tropical solar year was not 365.25 days as is presumed in the Julian calendar, but significantly shorter. In fact, the length of the solar year Is equivalent to 365 days, 5 hours, 48 minutes and approximately 46 seconds (or 365.242199). In the Julian calendar it is considered to be 365 days and exactly 6 hours long.

The Pope, who was greatly impressed by such an obvious inexactitude, decided to correct the calendar which had already been functioning very well for more than 1,200 years. In the Julian calendar, every fourth year is a leap year, i.e., three consecutive years containing 365 days are followed by a fourth year in which an additional day (the 29th) is added to February. In order to decrease the average duration of the year and to align it closer to the tropical (solar) year, the Pope decided to do away with certain leap years.

In the Gregorian reform, the leap year is abolished in centennial years which are *not* evenly divisible into four, that is in the years 1700, 1800, 1900, 2100, 2200, etc.. In the centennial years which *are* evenly divisible by four, the leap year is not abolished, i.e., 1600, 2000, 2400, etc.. Apart from this "correction", there are no other changes in comparison to the Julian calendar. In other words, every fourth year (except for those mentioned above) is considered to be a leap year coinciding with the Julian calendar.

What was the reason for making this "correction" and to what did it lead? Let's examine the words of explanation offered by Pope Gregory XIII himself in his famous Papal Bull *(decree)* "Inter Gravissimas", issued on February 24, 1582: *"Therefore we took care not only that the vernal equinox returns on its former date, of which it has already deviated approximately ten days since the Nicene Council **(325 – author)**, and so that the fourteenth day of the Paschal moon is given its rightful place, from which it is now distant four days and more, but also that there is founded a methodical and rational system which ensures, in the future, that the equinox and the fourteenth day*

of the moon do not move from their appropriate positions.".
It is hard to imagine that Pope Gregory XIII could not have
known that what he had expressed in his decree is, first of all,
absolutely impossible, secondly, absolutely unnecessary, and
thirdly, extremely detrimental.

All the prominent scholars of the time, including the great
Copernicus, adamantly refused to take part in the preparation
of this Gregorian reform. For everyone it was abundantly clear
that the length of a day, the length of a year and the length of
a month are quantities which are *not evenly divisible* amongst
themselves. In other words the result of dividing them
amongst themselves or even each individual quantity is always
an irrational number. Therefore, there can be no discussion of
absolute accuracy with regards to the calendar. Furthermore,
to establish something permanently, for instance that the
precise date of the vernal equinox and the 14th day of the
moon should never deviate from their positions, is absolutely
impossible mathematically. Even in the Gregorian calendar,
for example, the vernal equinox still shifts by an entire 24
hours every three thousand years.

But in general, no calendar has any inherent, essential value
in and of itself. Every calendar is viewed only from the aspect
of its ease of application. The practicality of calendar is its
most important asset, and not its abstract "accuracy". No
calendar can be "accurate", and the accuracy of any calendar
is always relative. Fortunately, this circumstance in no way
detracts from a calendar being beneficial and useful. That
same calendar which Pope Gregory undertook to correct had
been completely suitable for use for more than 1,200 years,
and the Pope's correction, although it provided an extra level
of relative precision for the solar calendar, proved itself to be
completely unsuitable for the Church.

The question arises, then what was that ancient calendar and to what purpose was it suited? That calendar was and is the Church calendar. It is the greatest accomplishment of ancient astronomy and one of the most brilliant masterpieces of calendar science. The fact is that the Church calendar is not simply the Julian solar calendar, as many nowadays think. The Church calendar only partly uses the Julian solar calendar in order to weave into one entity: first - the tropical solar calendar, secondly – the monthly cycle of the moon, and thirdly – the weekly cycle of days. This amazing merger into *one*, of three quantities that are mutually indivisible is one of the most brilliant achievements of astronomical science and is called the Church calendar, known as the "Paschalia".

In this Church calendar one cycle takes 532 years and one such cycle is called a "Peacemaking cycle". In this ingenious Peacemaking Cycle, all the inaccuracies in the mutual relations among the year, month and day of the week are mutually eliminated over the course of each cycle in such a manner that by the end of one Peacemaking Cycle and in the beginning of the next, the beginning point of a year, month, lunar phase and day of the week return almost exactly to their original. In other words, every 532 years, the Church calendar begins anew from the same point of origin each time.

From this point of origin when the beginning point of the year, month, lunar phase and day of the week coincide, the calendar again begins to unfold for another 532 years after which it again folds up into the same point of origin, but in a different time altogether. This amazing cyclic pattern describes a most beautiful spiral through time, and from an astronomical point of view is the only calendar which provides the possibility of uninterrupted chronology into both the past and future. Therefore the science of astronomy never could, nor would accept any other calendar, including, of course, the Gregorian calendar. Hence it was totally unnecessary and quite ridiculous to "correct" a calendar of such a high level of perfection and usefulness.

The damage that the Gregorian "correction" brought to astronomical science and to chronology became apparent from the very beginning and therefore, science could not accept the Gregorian calendar. But there is also a spiritual harm caused by this arbitrary foolishness, which merits examination.

Chapter Twenty Three —
The Spiritual Fruits of the Gregorian Reform

On the fourth day God created the sun, the moon and the stars and set them in the firmament of the heaven to give light upon the earth and to rule over the day and over the night and to separate the light from the darkness (Gen. 1). Their purpose was to separate the day from the night, and for signs and times and to form days and years. How much easier it is to keep track of days according to the rising and setting of the sun, and to keep track of months according to the new moon and half moon, than to keep accurate track of the passage of the solar year. Therefore, from the very beginning, mankind adopted the practice of orientating itself according to the days of the week and calculating the passage of time in months. Ancient calendars were based on the phases of the moon and calculated time in months; therefore the Old Testament calendar was a lunar calendar. Old Testament Passover was always celebrated on the day of the full moon in the first month of spring. The first month of spring was called Nisan, when the first grains for bread would ripen (also called Abib, the month of sheaths – Gen. 13:4). and in relation to the solar calendar it was the month of the vernal equinox.

Every month began on the evening when the first thin crescent of the moon would appear. The moon increased with each day (lunar epact) until the fifteenth day, after which the moon would wane until the thirtieth day. This is why on the fifteenth day the moon is always a full moon, and the Old Testament Pascha (Passover) was always celebrated on the 15th of Nisan, and the lamb was slaughtered and eaten on the eve of the celebration, that is on the 14th of Nisan.

In the year when Christ was crucified, the 15th of Nisan, the day of Passover, fell on a Saturday, and Christ was crucified on the eve of the feast, that is on Friday, the 14th of Nisan.

The entire purpose for celebrating the Old Testament Pascha was to *prepare* the Old Testament Church for the celebration of the *New Testament Pascha,* hence the transition from the Old Testament to the New Testament, is the transition from death to Life.

Therefore, the consecutiveness of the events of the Old Testament and New Testament Pascha are interconnected not only through their historic, chronological order, but most importantly through *spiritual* inheritance (succession) and the attainment of perfection. The sacrificial lamb is replaced by the Lamb Who descended from Heaven – the Heavenly Bread, and the Church and her members transition from their bondage not in Egypt, but their bondage in sin and death to the freedom of Truth and into the joy and abundance of eternal Life.

The day of the Resurrection of Christ – the new Pascha, became the primary and, therefore, central day of the entire life of the Church in a spiritual, liturgical and, consequently, daily sense. Right from the beginning, the Orthodox Christian lived and, to this day, lives from Pascha to Pascha and for Pascha. This Feast of all feasts illumined the entire universe, the entire Church, and each person, having proclaimed once and for all times the victory of Truth over falsehood, good over evil, life over death and light over darkness.

The day of the Resurrection (Sunday) became the first day of our new week (consisting of seven days) and in the Slavonic language was called "Nedelya" (non-working), for this was the day when people do not occupy themselves with earthly matters, but dedicate this new Sabbath to God. The Sunday of the feast of Pascha became not only the summit of the entire year, but also the central point of all our understanding and relation to time, i.e., the calendar.

The goal of the New Testament paschalians was to create a new understanding and relation to time and express this in a calendar of utmost perfection, reflecting the life and perfection of the Church of the New Testament. Therefore it became necessary to intertwine quantitative entities which previously had not been intertwined; the day, the week, the phases of the moon, the month and the solar year, but this had to be done in such a way as to correspond to the spiritual reality of the New Testament. For material reality is not detached from spiritual reality, but on the contrary, depends on it and reflects it to a certain degree.

Therefore it was necessary to design a calendar on which one could build the Paschalia in such a way that Pascha would always be celebrated only on a Sunday and not on any other day (as it had been in the Old Testsment); that Pascha would always retain its historic consecutiveness to the Old Testament Pascha on the 15th moon of Nisan, and simultaneously ensure that Pascha would always be celebrated only after the vernal equinox when daylight increasingly exceeds the darkness of night. Besides all of this, it was necessary to arrange the calendar in such a manner as to ensure that the New Testament Pascha henceforth would be completely independent of the Old Testament Pascha, just as a newly hatched chick no longer depends on the shell of the egg from which it has hatched.

And so it was, that the New Testament paschalians were able to achieve what A.N. Zelensky calls "the best achievement of human genius". The new Church calendar marvelously combined into one organic whole, both the rhythm of the material universe with the spiritual life of the New Testament Church. It provided science with a unique calendar, inimitable neither until then, nor ever after, which is the only calendar providing the means for a reliable, easy, uninterrupted, chronological calculation of all of history.

But most importantly, it beautifully expressed the height and perfection of Christian culture. It wholly illumined not only the entire universe but the overall and daily life of the Orthodox Christian. People lived the life of the Church. The life of the world was sanctified by the Church – it was a churched life. People lived from Pascha to Pascha. Over the course of the year life was regulated and defined by the majestic progression of Church feasts and fasts, which also revolved around Pascha. In this manner the Great Church Cycle of Paschalia (or simply the Great Indicon, as it was usually called), majestically bridled the elemental rhythm of the universe with the life of man, illumined by the imperishable light of the Resurrection of Christ, where the spiritual values of faith and truth prevailed over the darkness of unbelief and falsehood.

The Gregorian reform in the West undermined this entire structure. The Gregorian "correction" disrupted the simple rhythm of the Julian calendar and also disrupted the delicate and sensitive balance or symphony among the solar calendar, the lunar calendar and the seven day week. This crude absurdity destroyed any chance of synchronizing into one whole, the elemental movements of the sun and moon, and expressing them within the calendar flow of days, months and years. With the Gregorian calendar there can neither be a true Paschalia nor a Church calendar. Here any consecutive connection with the Old Testament Pascha was lost and life was deprived of its spiritual center.

In the Gregorian calendar, Pascha is celebrated randomly with regard to the Old Testament Pascha, either before or after it, and at times even coincides with it. But the celebration of Pascha either *before* or *on* Jewish Passover is strictly forbidden by the Church. It is precisely this manner of celebration that was in violation of one of the primary canons on the celebration of Pascha established by the Nicean Council itself in 325, which was of such concern to Pope Gregory in his decree. But the pope's concern was not over observance of the canon of this glorious council, but rather over merely *returning*

the position of the equinox and the 14th day of the moon to the same dates as those during the Nicean council, from which, as the Pope regretted, they had deviated.

It is not known why the Pope needed to *"return"* the position of the equinox and the 14th day of the moon, for they always must and, of course, will shift. But the Nicean paschalians arranged things in such a way that this shift occurs ceremoniously and in conformity with all calendars.

The Gregorian reform abruptly yanked only the solar calendar out of this organic whole, and even though it significantly enhanced its precision in comparison to the Julian calendar, it lost any possibility of an integral and correct understanding of time and relation to time.

But what was the spiritual damage caused by the Gregorian reform? It can be summed up in one word – *secularization*. Having lost the capability of the Church calendar, society also lost Pascha as the spiritual center of its life. Time ceased to be ordered according to the rhythm of Church feasts; now society became dependent simply on calendar dates. In a certain sense, man had now become dependent on time; no longer was time dependent on the spiritual life of the Church and on man.

Thus, society soon ceased to live the spiritual rhythm of the Church and basically began to live according to the secular life of dates. Church feasts, and primarily Pascha itself was shifted from the center of society's life to its peripheral rim. At its root, society became *unchurched* and ceased to recognize Church feasts properly; in estranging itself from the life of the Church, society immersed itself completely into the vanity of earthly life. The feasts and Church life remained only as a superficial cloak over society.

The Gregorian reform, of course, did not single-handedly cause such a turnover, but it contributed greatly to it and to a great extent was the catalyst for this transition in social orientation. As was already examined in the preceding chapters, during the course of these five centuries (from the 11th to the 16th) Western society had become entirely void of any spiritual foundation. Not only did it not comprehend the Church calendar, but long before that had begun to alienate itself from the calendar as something incongruous with their spiritual needs. Society simply was no longer capable of a true, spiritual, Church form of life. Quite simply, the Gregorian reform had finally severed the final thread which connected Western secular society to the Church.

But this did not really matter, for the spiritual body of papal society was already dead and its external tie to the Church was only burdensome for it. It had long been following its secular path and finally completely cut off from the Church (even if this had been through the calendar), it then lunged forward unrestrained, with greater ease, in the direction which the heart dictated. This deformed, spiritually useless new calendar completely corresponded to the spirit of those times. The calendar of Pope Gregory seemed for many at the time to be progressive. Meanwhile, progress at that time was becoming the new ideal. It had become the new pursuit of a new, reborn society, which had stepped onto the threshold of the age of enlightenment, the age of reason and, of course, progress.

CHAPTER TWENTY FOUR —
The Renaissance

It is commonly accepted to view the Renaissance era as something new, which radically changed the direction of society's development. It is commonly thought that the "Renaissance man" cast off stale theology, closed-mindedness, superstitious prejudice and finally opened his eyes and noticed the marvelous beauty and majesty of nature surrounding him, and, in particular, himself.

In actual fact, this was only a continuation, a natural development proceeding from the previous condition, comparable to a flower blooming from a bud, when the bud has matured, or like a chick hatching from an egg, not needing the shell any longer, ready to face the world by itself.

Humanism is a pseudo-religion which recognizes only one god – Man, and considers that man creates gods for himself according to his own image and likeness. This humanism began not with the Renaissance, but began entirely, if only unofficially, when the Pope of Rome separated from the Church, drawing away with him the majority of Western Europe. This separation has already been sufficiently dealt with in the previous chapters, but it must be emphasized that the religion of the man-god, even though it was already fully conceived, nonetheless remained in the fetal stage for the entire process of its maturation, throughout four centuries of scholasticism.

When the buds of humanism matured, the time for them to blossom had arrived. It was then, that the spirit of humanism began to manifest itself in complete openness in all aspects of human activity. In any artistic form; in painting, music, poetry and even theater, fallen man began to be celebrated pervasively in his fallen state, with all his flaws and passions.

From that time onward, the notion of man's (Adam's) fall and the total ruin and disruption of human nature completely disappeared from the horizon of the Western world-view. From that time on man began to think that "if God created me, then He created me just the way I am. If I have any shortcomings, then this makes me only more interesting and is in no way my fault and, besides, there is not much I can do about it. I don't need to repent so much but rather need to be celebrated"

There is, however, one aspect of the Renaissance era which should be further examined, for it served as the basis for an entire new system of thinking.

Until that time, mankind always had a teleological outlook on any and every phenomenon and on every object in the world. In observing any phenomenon, for example: "it is raining", upon asking the question "why?", man always understood this question from the sense of "for what purpose?". In other words, in any given phenomenon, its meaning and purpose was always perceived; hence, the congruity of purpose of the universe was always evident. Man always sensed not only the loving care of the Creator, but lived in peace of mind, knowing that God's Providence is always there in all things, even if we don't always see it clearly.

But as we have already discussed in a previous chapter, nominalism and reductionism completely overturned such an understanding. Now, when man would observe the very same phenomenon, upon posing the question "why?" he would tend to perceive this question in terms of "how?". Man now increasingly began to view all phenomena from the perspective of a chain of causality. The entire world and everything occurring in it was now viewed more in the capacity of a mechanism functioning according to the laws of blind cause and effect, in other words, any notion of the concept of *"willful origin"*, and consequently *"moral value"* was largely eradicated from all study of natural phenomena. While previously man would perceive the Providence of God and His loving care, purpose and meaning in things, modern man began to see only the mechanism, an endless chain of cause and effect and blind determinism.

Man ceased attempting to understand "why?", or "for what purpose?" and began to try only to understand "how?". In the absence of any determination of moral values, of good and evil, and having lost the concept of purpose or congruity of purpose, the Renaissance man became occupied exclusively with the pursuit of "how?". Thus, one may fundamentally identify that as a point of inflection in social consciousness, which is usually called the beginning of the contemporary, scientific world-view.

CHAPTER TWENTY FIVE —
Scientific Methodology

Contemporary scientific methodology is comprised of three parts. The first part is purely observational. This level is supposed to be a purely objective and dispassionate accumulation of individual empirical facts, without any distortion or interpretation. At this level, not only is any contribution from the individual who is gathering these observations not expected, it is not permitted. This creates the widespread impression that the scientist is an emotionally uninvolved observer, vested in a white dispassionate lab coat, a guardian of truth.

The second level of the scientific process is purely subjective and constructive and consists of the development of a theory. Here, not only is the creative contribution of the scientist permitted, but it is required. If, at the first level the scientist *discovers* empirical facts through careful observation then, at the second level, the scientist *invents* a theory which attempts to connect these facts. But this connection is originally imagined only by the scientist himself, who is inspired by rational perception to make a synthesis of the data and a guess at the actual reality behind his observations. Thus the theory always remains a creative product of the scientist's imagination, albeit based on his or her empirical observation. Therefore, Newton's theory of gravitation is just as much a creative work of Newton as the "The Map of the World" is the product of noted cartographer's Guillaume Delisle's informed and inspired imagination.

The following example may help to illustrate the point. The ancient Greeks had a theory of gravity. They supposed that every object has its natural "place". Heavier objects, such as rocks, belong "down" while lighter objects, such as clouds or hot air balloons, belong "up". When an object is displaced from its natural place, it then wants to return to it. The closer it gets to its natural place, or "home", the stronger the desire or pull it experiences to get there and so it accelerates. This is evident when one picks up a rock and then releases it. The rock will return to its natural place on the ground, accelerating as it goes.

This is an excellent scientific theory, based on empirical observation and quite useful within its scope.

A more sophisticated theory of gravitation was proposed by Sir Isaac Newton. Newton said that objects seemed to behave as if there was a force of attraction between them, which was directly proportional to their mass and inversely proportional to the square of the separation between them. It's important to note that Newton didn't say that there **was** a force, but that they behaved *as if there was a force* between them. So this *imagined* force Newton called "gravity". Newton's view of gravitational phenomena was also an excellent scientific theory based on empirical observation. It was very elegant and highly useful, within a certain range of applicability, especially since Newton invented a mathematical tool called "Calculus" to calculate all the parameters with relative precision.

Less than three centuries later Einstein came up with the theory of Relativity, which once again redefined our view of gravity. Einstein described gravity not as a force at all but as a curvature of space-time caused by the mass of objects present. This curvature or deformation of space-time is what causes objects to travel along their naturally curved geodesic (path) of the curved geometry of the local space-time. This view is strongly corroborated by the observation that photons, which have zero mass (and thus according to Newton would not be affected by gravity at all), nonetheless behave exactly like any other object that *does* have mass in a gravitational field as is indicated by Einstein's theory. In addition Einstein's view of gravity describes and explains the actual orbit of Mercury around the Sun, the precession of the perihelium of Mercury, as it's formally called. Newton's theory gives an incorrect calculation of Mercury's orbit that is at variance with actually observed fact.

Its is important to note that the ancient Greeks' theory of gravity was not "wrong" and Newton's theory was not "right". Neither was Newton's theory "wrong" and Einstein's "right" etc. any more than early maps of the North American coastline by Viking explorers were not "wrong" and subsequent maps by French and English explorers were "right".

And so, scientific theories are like maps of physical reality, similar to geographical maps of topography. In both cases, they are not themselves the actual reality but are *representations* of the actual reality. At first they are usually crude, but with time, they became more refined and more accurate and therefore more useful. But they never actually *become* the reality they represent, which always remains vastly more complex and subtle than any possible human representation of it.

The third level of scientific method is experimental. It involves performing experiments, which test the correctness of the theory proposed by the scientist. But this "correctness" is only relative and is assessed only by the ability of this theory to predict or presume a result, given certain specific conditions. The purpose of experiments always involves creating special conditions which would allow a new and often unexpected outcome or result. In this manner the theory itself is fine tuned and perfected or, in the extreme case, is completely replaced by a new theory.

If the theory withstands extensive testing and the results, which it predetermines, do not waver, then this theory is elevated to the level of "a law of nature". In physical nature, this would be categorized as a law of physics, in chemical nature, a law of chemistry, etc.

Contemporary scientific methodology is usually traced back to its founder, Francis Bacon (1561-1626). Bacon is generally considered to be among the first main critics of deductive syllogism (not so much deductive syllogism as an *a priori* unverified and unobserved basis of knowledge), which prevailed before his time for nearly 500 years in Western European scholasticism. But no matter how the process itself of deductive logic may have been accurate, its basic premise was always a given supposition. This basic supposition did not result deductively in and of itself, but was often an inaccurate and superficial impression. In his main work entitled "Novum Organum", i.e., "the new instrument" (for the acquisition of knowledge), Bacon proposes the inductive process for the collection of data, which in time began to be identified with the concept of "scientific method".

The inductive process is the accumulation of knowledge from empirically observed facts in order to create a basis for the body of knowledge. This differs from the scholastic approach, which draws conclusions based on *a priori* unobserved (previously accepted) facts.

In this inductive mode, a series of various facts which are evident to anyone through observation are put forward and united through various characteristics into a special grouping. Many differing phenomena, which at first glance seem to have nothing in common, can reveal a close connection in their very essence, for the experienced and contemplative observer who has closely examined them. Thus, many varied phenomena turn out to be one and the same elementary phenomenon revealed in various manifestations. Through this means, scientific exploratory methodology, by uniting various observations, in a way leads them (*inducts*-from the Latin *in ducto*) into one specific whole. This "whole" is then called a "hypothesis".

This hypothesis is then subjected to every possible experiment by the scientists in order to verify it. But to verify what? Its correctness? No. Its essence? Likewise no. They are verifying only the ability of the new hypothesis to predict a result within a specific and identical set of conditions. In this case, not only is there no question asked about "what is the purpose of this phenomenon?" but strictly speaking, in formal research methodology, the question "what is the purpose?" is not even appropriate. The only purpose is the probability of a definite and identical result given a specific and identical set of conditions. It is the ability of the experimental data to be reproduced by anyone at any time (under identical circumstances) that actually lends it credence and validity.

If the probability is great, then the hypothesis is called a "theory". The strength, or deductive value of this theory is only determined by its ability to statistically predict a result, given a definite set of conditions. So, in actuality, there is only a statistical foundation for all of modern scientific knowledge and not a deterministic, or cause and effect basis, as most "lay" people presume. There is no theory which can ever claim to have provided a complete explanation of the very essence of what is occurring. No "scientist" has or ever had any real idea even of what we call matter or what we call energy actually is, to say nothing of all the multifarious interactions that occur between them. Superstring theories now are attempting to make progress in this direction but they seem to be relegated to such an abstract dimension, so to speak, that they may have to be considered more philosophy than physical science.

This is why medical "studies" today invariably attempt to only establish statistical correlation between lifestyle or even genotype and certain health "issues" or even life expectancy and tend to shy away from any attempt to draw deterministic or direct cause and effect relations.

If an experiment happens to produce a different result than that which the theory had predicted, then the theory is modified in such a way as to include this new outcome. If the new facts are too contradictory, then the theory is abandoned and the development of yet another theory is begun.

It is this constant replacement of outdated theories by new ones, or the revision of old theories in order to modernize them, this is what constitutes the entire occupation and life of science in its most unbiased, pure and ideal definition.

But science, as such, is a purely human activity, a constructive and creative endeavor. And, since science does not exist in and of itself, but only in the person of its guardians – humans, then it follows that, in fact, it is subject to the same shortcomings which abound in the fallen nature of humans.

CHAPTER TWENTY SIX

The Cult of Science

From the moment that man was created by God, a strong instinctive desire to *understand* was implanted in his nature. In order to achieve this lofty goal, God gave man a bright mind, which imbued with the Holy Spirit (as it was in the beginning, before the fall), illumined nature and penetrated to a degree into the Wisdom of God, the Creator of all. When man rose up against God, the Holy Spirit departed from man, as a result of which the human mind was profoundly darkened.

Besides this, nature itself was cursed by God because of man, and also changed radically; it became foreign, forbidding and even hostile to man. From that time on, nature became fundamentally incomprehensible to man.

When someone sets out to study the work of a great master, like Beethoven or Rembrandt for example, they first try to understand the mind of the genius that created these works. They study the master's life and try to assimilate as much as possible the manner of thought and all the subtle nuances of character that would be reflected in the works, in order to better understand them.

God is not only all wise and omnipotent but He is also all holy. Everything that God does and creates reflects this holiness. When God created the world He did so in holiness, as sin had not yet entered into the world before the fall of Adam. To be able to begin to understand God's holy works a person must first begin to understand what holiness is. The opening words of the priest's prayer for the blessing of water is: "Great art thou, o Lord, and marvelous are thy works, and speech suffices not to sing the praises of thy wonders". Nature, as a creation of God, can only be properly grasped and fully comprehended by a dispassionate mind, one filled with the Holy Spirit - a holy mind, by a revelation from God Himself, the original Creator. But this knowledge and comprehension cannot be conveyed to a fallen mind, which is not enlightened by the descent of the Holy Spirit.

Science is a wonderful tool and it helps us understand many things, to a degree. It has made great strides in recent history and it empowers us to do very useful things as well as very harmful things. But science has very definite limitations in its field of operation. By its own mandate and definition science is limited only to the study of physical phenomena that can be perceived directly or indirectly through the five senses. This renders science completely inoperative in the realm of spiritual matters.

In matters of ethics, to answer the question "right or wrong?" science is not appropriate. With respect to values, "good or bad?" science cannot answer. With regard to morals, "virtue or sin?", "good or evil?", science is and must remain mute.

Almost every contemporary person believes firmly that science explains many things. And so it does. Many have the impression, however, that although there are some things that science cannot yet explain, it will however definitely do so in the future. And in general, there really is no such thing which science, in principle, is incapable of explaining.

But in fact, science does not explain even physical phenomena exhaustively and absolutely. Science has never explained nature completely nor will it ever explain it completely because, in the view of this author, the final full and complete understanding of nature is only possible *not* from a natural perspective, but from a supernatural perspective, from whence it was created. One simply cannot fully explain and understand a system from within that system and using that same system. This knowledge, or "pure knowledge" as Saint Isaac the Syrian calls it, is only possible for a mind in an exalted state of contemplation of the Divine, filled by the Grace of the Holy Spirit and in direct communion with the limitless mind of God. Not only did St. Isaac experience this state but St. Seraphim and St. Symeon – the new theologian, as well as many others in the history of the Church. In this state a person is able to see the creation of the world, the end of the world and the actual composition of material nature, among other things. But this knowledge cannot be conveyed to an ordinary fallen human mind regardless of its level of genius, because it's so far above and beyond even what we call "genius" now. It's in a spiritual dimension that we call "supernatural" now.

So of necessity, science lies in the realm of theories; and a scientific theory is essentially a map which is primitive but useful, which when made more accurate becomes more useful. As was already examined in the previous chapter, the sole purpose of science is to observe facts and build theories based on those facts. To philosophize, moralize or fully explain the essence of nature – all these are outside the realm of competence of science.

As was discussed earlier, modern scientific analysis came into being in large part due to a paradigm shift in intellectual consciousness from a teleological basis to a more mechanistic one. When intellectual inquiry shifted from a purpose-oriented one to a mechanism-oriented one the entire question of meaning became moot. Consequently modern science divorced itself de facto from questions of purpose and meaning, such as the purpose of rain or the sun or even the purpose of life, for instance.

Yet the desire to understand, to know, and in general *to be as God*, is naturally and deeply rooted in the soul of man, who was created in the image and likeness of God. And yet again, fallen and sinful man in general, refuses to accept this blessing freely from God, i.e., through Grace, but wishes to attain this on his own, independently. But a genuine understanding of nature, created by the Most Holy Mind of the Wisdom of God is likewise unattainable for fallen man, without the fullness of the Grace of the Holy Spirit, just as a genuine deification of man is impossible for him without Grace, no matter how hard he may try.

But despite everything, this does not deter man from such endeavors. And in the absence of real success in this area, man begins to persuade himself that he is indeed successful. With time, this imaginary success becomes more real for some than truth, and they begin to firmly believe in their imaginary successes.

It was in this manner that people began to believe that science is not merely a tool with a special but limited range of applicability and purpose, but that it is omnipotent and can and will explain and allow us to control all things. This view is called "scientism". Although in actual fact, science in and of itself, is quite a humble and humbling endeavor and does not presume to claim it has arrived at any exhaustive explanations. Good and honest scientists understand this well and attest to these things themselves.

Yet fallen mankind, again displaying its limitless ability to persuade itself through suggestion, has created an idol for itself out of the humble, purely observational instrument of exploratory science. Then it imbued this idol-science with limitless capabilities of explaining everything, what's more, subjectively and only according to the interpretation of that same fallen mankind. Thus, surrounding this idol of pseudo-science, the cult of science was formed.

The cult of science is seemingly based on science, but in reality it imprisons science and will not permit science to speak freely. Many real, honestly observed facts which science offers are interpreted by the cult of science and deciphered to suit its purpose. Facts which are impossible to be interpreted to suit one's purpose, the cult omits or conceals. Ideas that have not been scientifically tested, nor can be tested, are presented as established fact. Pure speculation is passed as solid scientific theory. This cult of pseudo-science has developed for itself quite a shrewd set of dogmas, which not only are not permitted to be changed, but are not to be questioned or doubted but are and must be accepted purely on faith. Many scientists who value their careers know well the limits beyond which neither study, nor observation, nor even discussion are permitted.

To the great sorrow of mankind, this cult of phantom-science has already raised many generations and now seems to have a firm grip in all of the "civilized" world. Access to genuine unbiased science is difficult because its not institutionally funded and accessible only to a very small part of the scientific population, largely to research scientists who are not prescribed a specific program, nor limited by a previously restricted framework for their endeavors. These are often quiet, humble, reserved individuals and often the world never hears or knows about them.

The majority of the population is served up something which has been extremely edited and mixed with very liberal slogans of dreamy fantasies under the guise of scientific accomplishments or discoveries, the entire purpose of which is to "scientifically" reaffirm that same humanistic and godless propaganda of which the contemporary world is now so full.

This is done predominantly through educational institutions, the entertainment industry and the media of the press, magazines, newspapers, but mainly, through television and now, of course, the internet.

The influence of this disinformation is most forcefully introduced via textbooks and programs of study in almost all contemporary schools and universities. In this manner, a situation has been created where contemporary society is convinced that it lives in the light of pure, unbiased scientific understanding and a scientific world-view.

In actual fact, the contemporary world is mired in not only spiritual darkness, but certain branches of "official science" have rejected the original tenets of scientific methodology and turned into a dead end, where likewise the darkness continues to increasingly thicken.

CHAPTER TWENTY SEVEN

The Age of Reason and Enlightenment

During the baroque period, and later on in the classical period, brilliant achievements in physics and mathematics brought Western European society into a state of unprecedented exhilaration. One of the main issues occupying the intellect of Europe at the time was the question: "what keeps the moon in its orbit around the earth?". For if one were to tie a rope to a pail and swing this pail around oneself, it is clear that the rope is what holds the pail in its "orbit". If one were to cut this rope, the pail would immediately fly off. But the moon is not tied to the earth with a rope, therefore the question arises, why does it not fly off?

At that time the plague was raging throughout Europe. All those who were able, fled from the populated cities to the countryside to avoid infection. One such privileged family in England was the Newtons; thus, young Isaac Newton became isolated for quite a lengthy period of time in the rural backwoods at a family estate without any contact with people.

Once, while he was observing apples falling from an apple tree, he inductively connected the idea of an object falling to earth with the idea of restraining the moon in its orbit around the earth (described above). At that moment he literally hit upon the notion of gravity, or gravitational pull, and later applied it to the theory of universal gravitation. But it was not only Newton who had discovered gravity, for this idea had been cropping up within the intellectual circles of Europe at that time. The problem was that no one could confirm it, or prove it in any satisfactory way.

To Newton's credit, without further delay, he invented the system of calculus, (that is the mathematics of integrals and differentials by using Riemann summations taken to limits of infinity), specifically for the purpose of verifying his conclusions on the theory of gravity. This was, however, complicated by the fact that he had no precise data on the mass of the earth and moon, nor on the distance between them. When he inserted these incorrect measurements into his new gravitational equations, which he developed with the aid of the integrals of calculus, they produced obviously erroneous results. Newton then decided that his theory was useless since it did not correspond to his observations, and he put away this work, which was scribbled on scraps of paper, into a box and gave it no further thought.

Some time later, when Newton was head of the faculty of mathematics at Cambridge University, he was approached for some advice by three most prominent European mathematicians and physicists. They wanted to know his opinion concerning the possibility of eventually solving the question of gravity through mathematics. Newton announced that he had already done so long ago, but apparently it hadn't worked. When they asked to see his work, he started to rummage through all his boxes, searching for the abandoned scraps of paper. One historian wittily noted that at that time all of Europe was seeking the answer to gravitation, when in the meantime Newton had lost it!

Finally, when these papers surfaced, the correct measurements were inserted into Newton's equations, and it turned out that they were quite correct. This marked the beginning of the new classical physics and mathematics upon which almost all contemporary technology is built.

In order to picture the enthusiastic reaction this generated in Europe, one needs only to mention the grand reception arranged in the English royal palace in honor of Newton. At the London cathedral in the solemn presence of European royalty and many dignitaries, a plaque was dedicated to Newton, inscribed with a special commemoration honoring the genius of Newton. This was a reformulated quote from the first chapter of Genesis:

"In the beginning there was darkness everywhere...

And God said: Let there be Newton!

And everything became light".

Indeed, Europe's enthusiasm knew no bounds. Discovery upon discoveries poured forth. The Kepler theories on the retrograde movement of the planets were finally established mathematically and fully confirmed. Newton's three laws of motion had formed the basis for mechanics and dynamics. It seemed that all the laws of nature were finally and completely exposed and understood. An obvious impression had emerged suggesting that the activity of the entire universe was almost completely understood and what was not yet understood, were mere trifles. The activity of the universe itself had become a mechanism.

It seemed to people that they had finally understood that the entire universe, from its very largest scale down to its smallest proportions, functions with precision, like a wound-up clock. Determinism prevailed throughout the world, and there was no longer a place or need in the world for God, except as a "prime mover", or as Newton expressed it, "the God of the gaps". For even in Newton's cosmology, he realized that there were certain gaps for which the existence of God would still be required.

Such a world-view, of course, is pure deism, and it was during this time that it became firmly enthroned in Europe.

CHAPTER TWENTY EIGHT —
Deism of the 18th Century

Deism completely refutes not only God's Providence in the world, but even all revelation from God, except for "natural revelation". Deism asserted that all the fullness of God's revelation is contained in the laws of nature. The deists maintained that, since God Himself is perfect, He has no need to constantly "interfere" through providence or miracles in the mechanism of nature, which He had created in an already perfect form. The very system of natural laws would execute the will of God and His Providence. Man must learn the laws of nature and live and act in accordance with those laws. Only in this manner could man fulfill the will of God, for the real and only laws of God were the laws of nature.

Among such laws of nature concerning the behavior of man, deism perceived as the law of seeking of pleasure and happiness, and avoiding pain and suffering. This law applied equally to all living beings. According to this natural law, each person had received from God not only the right, but even the obligation to seek happiness and pleasure and avoid suffering and pain. But for the deists this law applied exclusively to the material aspects of physical or psychological life, and not in the least to spiritual life, for deists denied spiritual life and in particular, the existence of hell.

It Is amazIng to what degree man's self-persuasion is capable of self-justification, in order to appease the conscience and give passions free reign. As has been noted earlier, man, without the help of God's Grace, is absolutely incapable of saving himself. In other words, **man himself is not capable of successfully struggling against his passions, and therefore turns to extremely shrewd "philosophies" in order to somehow avoid bearing moral responsibility for the knowledge of good and evil.**

This is why the deists did not tolerate either the New Testament, or the Bible in general, the concept of Grace or the sacraments of the Church. Deists often hated the Church and the clergy, and ridiculed them at every opportunity. But the "church" with which they were acquainted was not genuine, but a false one which, at the time, had already existed for over 700 plus years without Divine Grace which "heals the infirm and repletes the impoverished". And therefore, unfortunately, it had already become full to overflowing with all sorts of passions and debauchery. Yet within it there still remained some remnants of concepts from the Orthodox Church, and it was precisely these remnants of Christian ideology that the deists attacked most fiercely.

Here it is important to note that the deists, empowered by their law on seeking pleasure and happiness, and avoiding suffering and pain, were thereby essentially rejecting the concept of bearing one's Cross. The words of Christ: "whosoever wishes to be my disciple, renounce yourself and take up your cross and follow Me.", are completely rejected by the deists. They define deism as "enlightened self-interest". In other words, one may say that if someone wishes to be a deist, he must "reject the cross, take up his passions and follow them". It is interesting to note, that one prominent and open Satanist recently defined Satanism likewise as "enlightened self-interest."

But deism greatly contributed to the dream of building an independent paradise on earth, without God. Society, which was quickly advancing because of the progress of science, soon began to realize, that its social structure no longer corresponded to the spirit of the times. Monarchy, as a model of the hierarchical sovereignty of God over the universe was becoming increasingly foreign and unacceptable for a society which no longer felt that God was over it; it felt more a sense of its imaginary independence from God, and saw before itself an open field for activity toward its own "divinity".

Throughout Europe and especially in France and England, secret societies began to form, whose goal and activities revolved around the overthrow of the former structure and the establishment of a new one. The noble ideals, which had once been inherited from Christianity, based on love of God and of one's neighbor, on humility, abstinence and self-denial were brushed aside to make way for pride, self-love and the display of personal egotism. Social norms began to gravitate more and more towards the manifestation of the individual and independence. The relativism of Montesquieu, the deism of Voltaire, the skepticism of Hume and the naturalism of Rousseau ruled the minds of the majority of the intelligentsia in Europe and, to a significant degree, had begun to penetrate even Orthodox Russia, through the "window" which Peter The Great had recently hacked into Europe.

All the philosophy of the French "enlightenment" was building a sturdy foundation for open and complete godlessness and was relentlessly driving society toward revolution.

CHAPTER TWENTY NINE —
The Causes of Deism

Neither the French nor the Russian revolutions could have occurred if first an intellectual revolution had not occurred in the world-view of Western intelligentsia. In fact, by the 18th century, Europe, and particularly France, were boiling with socio-political philosophies, and the pressure from this ferment was on the verge of threatening to blow off the remaining frail membrane of an outdated and obsolete structure. In order to correctly comprehend and assess all of these cataclysmic events, it is imperative to understand the following.

The Church of Christ is the living body of Christ in which Christ Himself lives through the Holy Spirit. The Church has now two parts: the first – the Church triumphant, in Heaven; and the second – the Church militant, on earth. The earthly part, just as the heavenly, consists of many members, just as a body consists of many cells. But living in the fallen world, Her earthly members fall prey to numerous temptations, and in order to overcome temptations, each member must struggle with his passions. The battle against passions can only be successful with the abundant help of the Holy Spirit, Who lives in the Church, and creates an "immune system" (so to speak) within the living organism of the Church overall, and within every individual member. When one member, or even an entire part of the body of the Church rejects the Holy Spirit, and does not wish to repent, the Holy Spirit departs from it, and that part quickly begins to die spiritually. In order that this part not infect the rest of the body of the Church, it is cut off (similar to amputation), through the purposely established order of Anathema.

But the real harm begins when people who are spiritually blinded and in error follow such a "church", which could cripple them spiritually or completely mortify them spiritually.

This is what happened to the Roman Church, which cut itself off from the living body of Christ as early as the middle of the 11th century and dragged the western part of the Church behind it. And its flaws: pride, self-will, tortures, murders, the inquisition, burnings, wars, debauchery, indulgences and political intrigue, all of these, unfortunately, were simply the visible decomposition of a spiritually dead body. The love of power of the Roman church, its violent treatment of its population and the hypocrisy of its clergy only caused the people to be extremely perturbed by this injustice. The main thing was that the spiritual bankruptcy and the emptiness of the false-church would not, nor ever could, give the people true spiritual food which a rational soul requires. And so, the spiritual searching and needs of the people remained unfulfilled. On the contrary, a population which had been raised for already 700 years by such a "church" was crippled spiritually to such a degree, that even if they had wanted, many of them were already too paralyzed spiritually in order to come down on their own into the pool for healing.

It is not in the least surprising that the seekers of truth and justice of that time, although themselves also motivated to a significant degree by their passions and pride, no longer viewed that church as their authority, but even saw it as their enemy and oppressor. The people were doing the right thing by rejecting such a "church", but their main mistake and misfortune was that they did not set out to seek the genuine Church, unto Whom Christ Himself had promised invincibility until the end of time. Instead, these people began to invent their own philosophies, each according to his personal tastes and passions.

To its greatest misfortune, the West, in its majority, never did realize that the schismatic Roman Church was not the actual Church of Christ. People of Western upbringing continue to think that the Roman church is that same historic genuine Church founded by the Apostles, while the Orthodox Church is merely an eastern, more exotic version of the same church.

CHAPTER THIRTY

The Consequences of Deism

In mid 18th century Europe, the atrophied institutions and regulations of the antiquated establishment, experienced ever increasing attacks from the "enlightened" intelligentsia. Voltaire, who personally became the target of much humiliation and vexation at the hands of the Parisian aristocracy, protested loudly against the despotism of the monarchy, aristocracy and church. From his place of exile in England he was developing the idea of religious pluralism which contributed to the future development of ecumenism. He said, for example, that if there is only one religion in the country, then it would unavoidably be despotic. But, if there were two religions, then they will always fight each other. However, if there be thirty religions, as for example in England, then they will all peacefully coexist amongst themselves.

In general, among the foremost thinkers of this era, the notion of the absolute had completely vanished, except for the absolute of empirical facts, given meaning and sense by a rational process of logic. But not only had the notion of an absolute, only, true religion been done away with, relativity began to penetrate into all aspects of life.

Montesquieu (Charles-Louis de Secondat, Baron de Montesquieu, 1689-1755) had traveled extensively throughout many distant countries and was amazed at the variety of cultures. He wrote a work entitled "Persian Letters" in which he harshly satirized all European culture in general with all its institutions. His literary works received a broad audience throughout Europe and under their influence, Europeans began to dabble heavily in the exotic. It became fashionable to be infatuated with foreign cultures; Indian, Chinese, Japanese, Arabian, and the European's imagination was particularly captivated by the American native Indian.

A strong sense of arbitrariness emerged in the abstract equality of all cultures. The humdrum of daily life and the ancient customs of Europe, which had predominantly been formed on Christian values, completely lost their authoritativeness.

The book by Caesar Beccaria (Caesar Bonesana, Marquis di Beccaria) on indispensable legislative reforms, created a furor in Europe. He insisted on the equitable application of the law to all individuals regardless of their social status and not according to a judge's discretion. Beccaria protested against cruel punishment and demanded that the punishment for any crime be not a tool of revenge but a minimal measure for correction.

But what resulted in perhaps the most important consequence, was Beccaria's demand that any spiritual or religious crimes be eliminated from the law altogether. Such were, for example, blasphemy, sacrilege, heresy, etc., which prior to that could have incurred the harshest punishments. In general, Beccaria demanded that all "religious" crimes should be left up to God, so that He would deal with His transgressors, according to His discretion. But the state law, according to Beccaria, should deal exclusively with civil matters, and as such, must be completely secular.

Incidentally, Beccaria was proposing a well known principle of civil legislation, based on the indisputable right of each member of society to pursue his own personal happiness, but by doing so, not infringe on the right of other individuals to do likewise and cause no grief or harm to other members of society.

The main results of Beccaria's reforms were two-fold. On one hand, the concept of sin was separated from the concept of crime, thereby opening up the field for the spread of amoral activity which was not subject to legal scrutiny. Such activity included not only heresy and sacrilege, but also various forms of fornication, perversion and all "unnatural" sins. In this manner, the entire concept of "sin" was doomed to gradually become extinct in the abstract and subjective spheres of individual and social consciousness.

On the other hand, Beccaria's separation of religious crimes from civil law contributed to the imminent separation of state and church.

All of this prepared the groundwork for forthcoming revolutions and the establishment of a new, secular order. But as every stone edifice is built one stone at a time, likewise, each of these "stone masons" contributed his own stone in the building of the new secular order.

Rousseau made his contribution by disagreeing totally with all culture and civilization. He is therefore considered to be a prototype of the "hippy" movement. An ardent deist, Rousseau introduced the concept of "artificiality". Not only did he revolt against everything spiritual as did every deist, but he also rebelled against anything that was not natural, which he called "artificial".

Rousseau argued that all the evil in the world comes from human works and civilization in general, for example, cities, buildings, human institutions, religion, books, culture, fashion, etc. He asserted that the development of each civilization invariably leads, in the final analysis, to the perversion of life and morals and to complete moral degradation. The only correct path for man, according to Rousseau, is to return to a primitive condition, without any personal property or monogamous marriage, etc. From this, the concept of the "noble savage" originated, whose image so captivated the imagination of future generations in the literary works of James F. Cooper, Henry D. Thoreau and other authors.

But then, on November 1st, 1755, a powerful earthquake shook Europe, almost completely destroying the city of Lisbon. The extreme scale of this indescribable tragedy, which caused tens of thousands of casualties, had a profound impact on Voltaire and other free-thinkers and would change the future course of the intellectual life of Europe.

Seeing such a colossal tragedy, Voltaire wrote a poem of compassion on that occasion, which circulated throughout Europe. Voltaire concluded that abstract philosophy, in and of itself, has no value, but the sole purpose of philosophy and any knowledge in general, was in its application for the purpose of alleviating human suffering. Since then, all knowledge and philosophy began to be viewed only from a utilitarian perspective, i.e., according to the extent of benefit they might bring mankind.

Philosophical ideas, as such, ceased to be offered to the public directly, but began to be incorporated into the form of literary works, poems, novels, etc.. The gaze of European intelligentsia became fixed on writers who dealt with the paramount daily issues of life in their literary works.

Then all of this ferment began to ripen and soon yielded fruits worthy of itself: Revolution. At this point it is not necessary to delve into the details of the French revolution, as it has been discussed in detail in many noteworthy works. Nonetheless it is appropriate to note that despite everything that is said to the contrary, not one revolution, including the French revolution, did occur spontaneously on its own because of a distressed, oppressed population rising up spontaneously in rebellion against their oppressors.

Revolution was conducted in the most driven, intentional and truly "artificial" manner. Very much money, ability and perseverance was invested by individuals and parties in their own interests in order to force common French folk to rise up against their faith, king and homeland.

CHAPTER THIRTY ONE —
Naturalism and Materialism

The spirit of atheism had already been drifting across Europe for a long time, but it always remained a concealed and subtle current. Having arrived at deism, Europe was not quite prepared for the next step – the complete denial of God. Although the belief of the deists in their "God" certainly had nothing in common with the true Faith and the true God any longer; the deists could not yet simply part with it altogether for two reasons:

First of all, they said, inanimate matter cannot move by itself, but is put into motion by other matter, which is already in motion (like the action of billiard balls). But since the entire universe is already in constant motion, some sort of *immaterial origin* of all this motion must therefore exist. Such a source of all motion must itself be not material, but spiritual and indicates the existence of a spiritual origin – God, the "Prime Mover", as they called Him.

The second reason for faith in God, according to the deists, remained the problem of self-willed motion. According to their reasoning, any animate creature, and particularly man, could move about at will and even initiate a chain of movements, but this was only because the subject creature was *animate*, i.e., consisting of not only a material body but of a soul as well. The argument for the existence of the soul was that it was capable of willing and affecting the movement of inanimate matter, and therefore, the soul itself must also be not material, but spiritual.

In this manner, although European society had deeply immersed itself in deism, it nonetheless firmly clung to the *idea* of God as the Creator (prime mover) and to the idea of an immortal soul. Atheism was still disdained as being ridiculous, bordering on madness. But by the middle of the 18th century, atheism began to emerge more openly and boldly in the figure of Doctor Julien de la Mettrie.

De la Mettrie (1709-1751) was a French physician who wrote "L'homme machine", that is "Man the Machine". In this book he attempted to prove that it is not the soul which controls the body, but on the contrary, the body rules the soul. According to Mettrie, the soul in and of itself, is only an "affect" produced by the physiological functions of the body and in actual fact no "soul" exists. He used the argument that when the brain is damaged, the soul is also damaged, while when the brain recovers, the soul also recovers. When the body is afflicted, then the soul is also downcast, but when the body is enjoying something, the soul likewise rejoices.

Incidentally, De la Mettrie reduced the entire purpose of life to the acquisition of happiness, just as the deists, but the former understood happiness in a very narrow sense – bodily pleasure, while later deists understood "happiness" as more of a "psychological" well-being, not purely physical. Despite the fact that De la Mettrie was not acceptable to Europe of that time, European society nevertheless preoccupied itself with his book "Man the Machine", and his endeavors firmly entrenched themselves in the groundwork of the atheism which later followed. His teaching built a new, amoral set of ethics on the foundation prepared by Beccaria in the latter's legalistic writings.

De la Mettrie taught, for instance, that self abuse or homosexuality are not harmful, and only supposedly bring pleasure, and therefore happiness. Therefore, according to him, no fault can be found in such actions, and there was nothing wrong with them. Faults, or crimes, according to his interpretation, were such actions which bring harm to society, or damage to an individual and simultaneously, in and of themselves are not beneficial. The aforementioned behaviors, according to his teachings, brought no one any harm, only pleasure to the participants, and therefore, according to Beccaria they are not a crime, while according to de la Mettrie, they are not faults.

The concept of sin remained only within the "unenlightened" uneducated lower classes and in the "outdated" institution of the church. The "enlightened" society had already begun to depart from the notion of "sin", in an attempt to drown its conscience and to permit their passions free reign.

Yet, de la Mettrie was finally exiled from France, and the Prussian King Fredrick accepted him in his court in order to spite the French court. But in Frederick's court, de la Mettrie soon succumbed to food poisoning from spoiled pâté and died suddenly, to the glee of all Europe. However, de la Mettrie's ideas penetrated deeply into European thought and the road to atheism significantly broadened.

CHAPTER THIRTY TWO

The Threshold of Atheism

Denis Diderot (1713-1784) was the head of the French encyclopedists, and himself was a total atheist. But he concealed his atheism from the general public, and only preached it openly in the Parisian salons. He asked that his letters on the subject of atheism not be published until after his death so that they might not damage him personally.

Diderot taught that essentially there is no difference between an animate being and an inanimate object. He attempted to prove that living and dead objects actually consist of the very same matter. In order to prove that a living person and a stone statue of that same person are one and the same matter, he offered the following explanation. He proposed that a stone statue be ground to dust, then the dust be mixed with clay and water; then a vegetable be planted in the mixture, which is to be eaten by a living person and in this manner the person could ingest the matter of the statue, thereby incorporating (literally) the material of the statue into his own living organism.

Through such penetrating insight Diderot then became worthy of further inspiration! If he could turn stone statues into living persons step by step, he imagined that in general all living (not stone) animal species could gradually become each other (transform themselves from one into another). He himself wrote then that he did not know at the moment when this thought suddenly illumined his mind, whether this was a profound matter, or just sheer madness. One could probably agree with him on both counts!

But Diderot continued to develop this thought further and finally arrived at proto-evolutionary contemplation. He suggested the idea that all animals are constantly evolving and only the environmentally fittest survive, while the others die out. He decided that this process of evolution required millions of years, but at that time the commonly accepted age of the earth was understood to be approximately 7,000 years. Diderot suggested that if one were to replace the understanding that the earth was 7,000 years old with the idea of several million years, then there would be no obstacle to the idea that in general all of life is of independent origin.

Finally Diderot even concluded that each cell in the human body contains everything which is necessary for the recreation of the entire body. One can only imagine how astonishing this idea was for that time, if one considers that the science of genetics was only discovered one hundred years later and the concept of "cloning" not till much later still. But Diderot, inspired by the spirit of "clairvoyance", even jested that the time would come when one could enter a store and select from a shelf, like a bottle of wine, a cell from the body of any poet from a specific era (in order to re-create that poet --auth.), knowing in advance that this was a good year for poets!

By the end of the 18th century, the winds of atheism began to blow ever stronger throughout Europe and by the beginning of the 19th century it bore down with much greater force on the aging and crumbling world-view of European culture. But for now, it could not yet blow down faith in God the Creator because, after all, the majority of the population, and even the intellectual elite, differentiated between what was alive and what was dead and could not in any way comprehend how life could occur *in and of itself* from a non-living origin, or how animals could transform from one into another. But mainly, man was not yet considered to be merely one of the animals, or consisting of only dead matter and nothing more. Man, after all, did still occupy a special, separate position in the animal kingdom, possessing not only rational and creative capabilities, but a conscience as well. And it was that conscience which would not leave this brand new man in peace.

This is why such a man viewed atheism with what seemed like a longing, but still was cautiously fearful of it and did not know quite how to latch onto it, for it seemed that in atheism it would finally be possible to hide from God. But how one could swallow this atheism remained uncertain. Besides, the main thing was that for now it was simply not appropriate to be openly atheistic in cultured society.

CHAPTER THIRTY THREE —
The Embryonic Stage of Evolution

"Be not afraid of them that kill the body, and after that have no more that they can do", warns the Saviour, *"But I will forewarn you whom ye shall fear: Fear him, which after he hath killed hath power to cast into hell; yea, I say unto you, Fear him."* (Luke 12:4-5)

No matter how horrifying the French Revolution was, yet for the most part it had unfolded on a physical level. But its famous architects, primarily Voltaire, Rousseau and Diderot, laid the foundation of yet another, significantly worse revolution, which occurred only one hundred years after them, but drew behind it countless millions of human souls into utter darkness.

Diderot's proto-evolutionary musings circulated throughout Europe for nearly 100 years, seeking an opportunity to embody themselves into a concrete idea. Similar thoughts were also disseminated by Buffon, Condorcet and Lamarck. But on their own, these ideas were as of yet powerless to ignite people's imagination. Hydrogen, for instance, does not burn on its own but requires oxygen to create combustion and fire.

The French philosopher, Lamarck (1744 – 1829) was a private tutor of Count Buffon's children. In the frequent discussions held in the Buffon home, Lamarck had heard extensive speculation on the evolution of the species. Lamarck provided a more tangible form for this speculation. He postulated, that physical changes acquired by any organism over the course of its life are passed down inherently to the next generation.

He explained, for instance, that throughout their lives, giraffes stretched out their necks in order to reach ever higher leaves on trees, and therefore they produced offspring with longer necks. Hence, over time, giraffes developed long necks. Or another example was a blacksmith, who would use his right hand to strike the steel, would therefore develop large muscles on his right arm; consequently his son would be born with an exceptionally strong right arm. Although these fantasies of Lamarck were ridiculed by French scientists of the time, nonetheless they continued to circulate throughout Europe.

Voltaire is considered to be the initiator of another idea, which he conveyed to his admirer, the American Benjamin Franklin when the latter was visiting Voltaire in France. Franklin included this idea in his book entitled "Miscellany" (pg. 9) where eventually it was read by Malthus.

Thomas Robert Malthus (1766-1834) expanded this idea in his literary work entitled "An Essay on the Principle of Population" which was published in 1798. This idea consists of the following: the ability of any population to multiply far exceeds its ability to obtain its sustenance. In other words, in every living species, including mankind, a far greater number of offspring can be born than can possibly survive because of a perpetual shortage of food. Because of this, there is a perpetual and unavoidable struggle for survival.

It follows, therefore, that a significant portion of any population always dies of starvation, and only the strongest and most adaptable ones survive. This would mean that throughout all times and places the corpses of many individuals of any population would be strewn about – deer, birds, camels, people, etc., which gradually died of starvation, having lost the battle for the last bit of food.

Malthus himself did not observe any such thing, but only referred to Franklin's book. The majority of Europe, likewise had not encountered any such thing, and over the following thirty years spoke out very strongly against Malthus. Nevertheless, this idea did create a very strong impression and some scientists launched a search for its proof, or at least for similar cases.

Malthus studied some mathematics, but the bulk of his education was at the spiritual academy of Cambridge in order to become a village priest, or "parson". While ministering in a small parish, Malthus compiled his thesis even though he had not studied biology at all. He based his essay primarily on observing the population growth of America as compared to England. Yet he pervasively applied his conclusions on the shortage of food and resulting struggle for survival to both the entire zoological and botanical worlds.

Yet every search for examples of this fantasy would prove completely futile and even contrary to expectations. Even after one hundred years, in 1902, the scientist Peter Kropotkin wrote in his book "Mutual Aid", that no matter how hard he had tried to find at least something like this in nature, in the end he found nothing of the sort. But, on the contrary, he found that among animals of any species, mutual aid and support prevailed throughout. As, for example, in the case of penguins taking turns to break the wind for the entire flock in cold, windy conditions.

In the same vein, the director of the department on animal population at the Oxford University wrote, that after a lengthy study they found that the number of any animal population almost never reaches the limits of established food supply. Furthermore, in general there are almost no cases of death from starvation in the animal world.

None of this, of course, implies that population size is not at all related to food supply. Populations generally do tend to increase as food supply increases and populations do recede as the food supply shrinks. But the decrease of the population is not caused by individuals systematically dying off from hunger, unable to compete with their stronger and more aggressive peers. There are many other mechanisms built into population controls such as decrease of litter size and birthrate, for instance, during times of hardship or environmental duress. These are all ways that God, the loving Creator, has taken care of all His creatures, that none of them go wanting.

Competition for survival and survival of only the fittest is an idea that does have some merit actually, but it only insures that the degenerate, or "mutant" specimens are weeded out, in order to preserve the species as a whole in a stable and healthy state, certainly not to "evolve" it into a new and different species.

At this point it is appropriate to remember the words of the prayer before mealtime taken from the Psalm of King David: "The eyes of all look to Thee in hope, O Lord, and Thou givest them their food in due season, Thy openest Thy bountiful hand and fillest every living thing with Thy favour.", as well as the words of the Saviour Himself when He speaks of birds which do not sew nor reap, but not one of them is forgotten by God, Who feeds them all. In this matter, one often hears objections, citing famines or the "overpopulation" of China or India, etc.. For the sake of accuracy and fairness, one must emphasize that famines are not a constant, normal state of the entire animate world, as Malthus taught, but are extraordinary occurrences within the *human* world, often caused maliciously by depraved individuals for political or selfish economic purposes, or at least by the criminal negligence or carelessness of humans. In any case, famines are sometimes *permitted* by God in order to bring humans to their senses and correct them. But in the animal world, God 's system of accountability is different. In it, God established an extremely delicate balance in the food chain, the disruption of which (usually by humans) results in serious consequences.

Malthus also attracted much other criticism for the frequent extremely harsh comments he made in his writings, such as: "An infant has relatively little value for society, since, without a doubt, his function is supplanted by others; his main value consists in being the center of one of the greatest passions of human nature: that of parental tenderness." Malthus also wrote that an orphan, or for that matter any human whose family is unable to support him, has no right to receive food or any other aid from society, for nature itself has already doomed him to destruction and would soon carry out its sentence.

It was probably noticed at the time, that the spirit of Malthus was somehow not quite suited to being a parish pastor, nor did his knowledge measure up to the stature of a biologist. Therefore, not long after the release of his book "An Essays on the Principle of Population", Malthus was transferred to the post of professor of "political economics" (a new position, created just for him and the first such post in English history) in an obscure college bearing the name "Eastern India", in the village of Hertfordshire, where he managed to stay until his own death in 1834.

Malthus was also considered to be the founder of the contemporary practice of birth control. At that time, the population of England was 12 million, and Malthus demanded an immediate halt to the growth of England's population, since otherwise it would be impossible to feed all the people. But in 1940, the population of England numbered more than

47 million, almost four times greater and no one was dying from hunger.

Nevertheless, Malthus' idea had a strong impact in Europe's atmosphere where Lamarck's idea on the hereditary inheritance of adaptations to one's environment was already making strides. Both these ideas were a total fabrication of human imagination and were not based on any scientific observations. They were quite ridiculous in and of themselves, and even represented a certain insult to human reason and sobriety, as well as a certain harmfulness to morality. But their main potential lay in their union, like for instance, that of hydrogen and oxygen. And so, they wafted throughout the intellectual atmosphere of Europe, as if seeking each other, or better said, seeking a person whose imagination could unite them.

The wait was not long. Fifteen years later, in 1813, Doctor V.S.Wells delivered a lecture to the English Scientific Society, the "Royal Society", on the topic of "evolution", on the means of "natural selection". Then, again, in 1831, a certain Mr. P.Matthew included that same idea in the appendix of his book "Naval Timber and Arboriculture". But no one paid particular attention to them and there was no intellectual "explosion". Something was lacking. Perhaps there was not yet a critical mass or simply a suitable individual.

CHAPTER THIRTY FOUR —
Darwinism

Karl Darwin (1809 – 1882) was born in the wealthy home of his father, a well-known English physician and spent a calm and carefree childhood. He did not display any unique abilities and was indifferent to books and learning. He made an attempt to study medicine in his father's footsteps, but quit after two years, finding it exceedingly boring.

Then his father placed him in theological school, which Karl completed in 1831. But Darwin felt no calling to be a parson of a rural parish, and his friend, G.S.Henslow secured a post for him aboard the ship "Beagle" in the capacity of a naturalist. The "Beagle" set sail on December 27th of that same year, 1831, on a five-year voyage around the world. Darwin's duty was to record in a diary the details of all the animals and plants, which they would encounter.

Darwin was astonished at the enormous variety of flora and fauna in the world. Within every species there were so many types. In every type there were many strains – countless variations of specific specimens. But Darwin himself did not know what a "species" was, and incidentally, he wrote that no naturalist knows for certain how to define the meaning of a "species". And indeed, at that time, until Mendel discovered genetics, the naturalists could not find a definition for "species", except for that which relates to "ancient and unknown concepts of Creation", as Darwin expressed it. And these "ancient and unknown concepts of Creation" suddenly became quite odious. It was then, that Darwin decided that "species" as such, do not exist at all, but there exist only specimens with countless variations. "It is impossible to distinguish strains, or variations from species", wrote Darwin, "except that there are greater differences among species than among strains." For example, among the strains (breeds) of dogs (German Shepherd, Dachshund, etc.) there is a difference, but between the species of cats and horses, the difference is far greater. In comparing the *difference* among dogs and the *difference* between dogs and cats, Darwin decided that it was simply a matter of degree. In other words, it seemed to Darwin that the difference between species and strains was not qualitative, but simply quantitative.

This of course, is nothing more than pure nominalism. But nominalism was a philosophy, whereas Darwin applied it to nature in the absence of knowledge or understanding of science. According to Darwin, this meant that bears or deer do not exist; only four-legged animals which vary from each other exist. But since there are also similarities among them, it is *we* who define them as bears, deer, etc., at our own discretion.

Obviously Darwin did not study the Bible very well while he was enrolled at the theological academy. For in the very first chapter of the Bible, Moses wrote through the Holy Spirit: *"And God made the beast of the earth each **after his kind*** (emphasis.-auth.) *and cattle **after their kind,** and everything that creepeth upon the earth **after his kind**: and God saw that it was good."* (Gen. 1:25). Throughout the Book of Genesis where there is reference to creation, the phrase *"after their kind"* is added. This is extremely important, and this is why it is repeated throughout. In the first chapter of Genesis, *"after their kind"* is repeated **ten times**: three times when referring to vegetation; two times for fish and birds, and five times for land creatures.

The species were created by God exactly, each in a distinctive and unconfused form. In nature this remains as one of the most durable laws and immutable concepts. The key to understanding a "species" lies in the very word "species" or "genus", that is being born of parentage, i.e., the same issuing forth from the same. In the contemporary definition of genetics, a species is a mutually reproductive (interbreeding) pool of genes. A species is defined not so much morphologically (the science of forms) as *genetically*. Any species is comprised of those animals which are able to breed and reproduce amongst themselves, as God had commanded them. Animals, the DNA of which is not compatible, cannot reproduce, and therefore belong to a different species.

Unfortunately, Darwin simply did not know this, for genetics was discovered later by Mendel. It was only by 1862 that Mendel published his wonderful scientific study on the transfer of physical characteristics to offspring exclusively by means of genes inherited from the parents, but amazingly, his work was ignored and remained in obscurity for forty years until the beginning of the 20th century.

But Darwin was a gifted dreamer and no matter how disturbed he was by a shortage of knowledge and absence of facts, he, nevertheless would not be held back. Upon his return home to England in October of 1836, Darwin began to contemplate his impressions. He undertook the breeding of pigeons, artificially augmenting the differences among their breeds. He was astounded by the variety of breeds and decided that these were no longer various breeds of pigeons, but actually new species of birds. But, of course, they were still pigeons and did not become a different type of bird, and of course, continued to breed amongst themselves. And if they were left to breed freely, then all the extremes in the breeds would become intermingled and even out within the vast range of pigeon genes.

But Darwin did not understand this and decided that he was producing new species of birds rather than simply extreme breeds of pigeons. He knew that he had achieved these extreme variations through artificial and deliberate means. Now his objective, as he perceived it, was to establish how this occurs within nature. What process of *selection* occurs in nature to produce new breeds, and, therefore, new species. Darwin wrote in his letters: "But how the process of selection was applied to organisms in their original state remained a mystery to me for a certain while." ("Life and Letters", p.83).

Darwin suddenly "saw the light" in October of 1838 when he read that famous (or infamous) work of Malthus, "An Essay on the Principle of Population" discussed earlier in this work. Despite the fact that Darwin himself had spent five years carefully observing the animal world, he had not ever encountered such an idea. Darwin had sailed the entire world and observed animals for five years and never had the idea occurred to him that everywhere, as a rule, all animals fight each other to the death for a last scrap of food which can never be sufficient for all, and therefore many of them die of hunger.

Darwin was no stranger to the art of self-persuasion. In his book, "Origin of the Species" (Chap. 3), he writes: "De Candol and Lyell have proven generally and philosophically, that all organic beings are subject to fierce competition". Further on, he continues, "There is nothing easier than accepting this at its word, yet, there is nothing harder than constantly maintaining this conclusion in one's mind, or at least in my case."

From Malthus' book, Darwin extracts not only a philosophical, but a "mathematical" proof. Malthus wrote that any population can grow "geometrically", that is with each generation it increases twofold, then 4, 8, 16, 32, etc., yet food could only increase "arithmetically", by twofold, then by 4, 6, 8, 10 times, etc.. In an attempt to explain that it is actually so, Malthus adds, "I simply cannot imagine that food could increase at a faster rate than this".

Darwin, who never studied this kind of mathematics, as Malthus apparently had, was completely convinced through this mathematics, of the inevitability of a universal struggle for food and death by starvation for the losers. Thus, Darwin cites this "mathematics" as proof of the latter in his book (Chap. 3).

Yet twenty more years passed and Darwin still could not bring himself to publish this conjecture. He carefully concealed it within himself and revealed it to no one, fearing he would be ridiculed. He was well aware that he had not a single example, not one fact, nor one observed case. He was constantly plagued by terrible doubts, that all of this is sheer nonsense and, as he wrote two days before the publication of his book, "Frequently a cold shudder penetrates me and I ask myself: could I have devoted my entire life to a fantasy?" (Life and Letters", p.229). At the time he had written to his friend, Huxley, "I had horrible premonitions, and I thought, what if after all I had been fooling myself as had many before me?" (ibid, p.232).

But then an unexpected crisis occurred. In June of 1858, Darwin received in the mail the written work of Alfred Wallace, which the latter asked Darwin to read in front of a scientific society. Darwin glanced at this work and nearly fainted, for it was a complete copy of his own idea on evolution through the process of natural selection, otherwise known as the survival of the fittest.

Wallace was a young naturalist who was on an expedition to the East Indies. He also happened to read Malthus' articles "On Populations", and he immediately sat down and drafted the exact same idea on evolution with which Darwin had already been struggling for twenty years. Wallace had come to this notion by precisely the same path as had Darwin, that is through philosophical, not scientific means. He took his data also from Malthus' book, rather than through observing empirical facts within nature.

Darwin was gripped with yet a greater fear – that he would be outdone, and that his thoughts would therefore not be original. Immediately, Darwin hurriedly wrote his own version of the same work on evolution and on July 1, 1858 he read his own composition together with that of Wallace in front of the Linnaean Society of London. The lecture was delivered under the patronage of two foremost British scientists, the geologist Charles Lyell and the botanist, J.D.Hooker.

Wallace very kindly conceded to Darwin the honor of authorship of this idea, stating that his own personal effort took only two weeks, while Darwin had already labored over it for twenty years. Besides, Wallace was located at the other end of the globe at the time and did not wish to compete with Darwin, particularly over some conjecture.

But Darwin no longer lost any time. He hurriedly undertook the writing of his book "Origin of the Species" which he finally completed and released by the end of the following (1859) year. Shortly before the release of his book, a close friend of Darwin's and his main propagandist, Huxley, wrote his own glowing commentary on the book, which the newspaper "The London Times" published in its December 25, 1859 issue, occupying an unprecedented entire three and one half columns. Ironically, "evolution" was officially "born" on December 25th.

The first edition of Darwin's "Origin of the Species" was entirely sold out on the very first day. Second and third editions immediately followed and were likewise immediately sold out. This book changed the world once and for all, as well as its future course. The world was thoroughly delighted.

CHAPTER THIRTY FIVE —
Evolution

Evolution is a philosophical idea and must only be accepted purely on faith. Evolution is not a science and is not based on a single fact or observation or on any scientific process. It is based on the entirely false idea of Malthus about the perpetual universal shortage of food, and on the completely false idea of Lamarck concerning the inheritance of physical changes by a new generation from a previous generation. These two pillars on which the fantasy of evolution was originally built, in and of themselves, are likewise, in no way scientific, but are purely abstract and philosophical.

Adaptation is often confused with evolution. Adaptation is a fact and it's quite real. Evolution is a myth and does not exist in reality at all, only in fantasy. There is a fine line separating them.

Adaptation is when an individual or a species collectively changes to adapt to their environment. Such changes can be subtle or very striking. The changes are physical (phenotype) and, in the case of an *individual*, can be brought about in a direct response to a stimulus from the environment. An example of this is a suntan, or the strong right arm of a blacksmith, to use Lamacrk's example. These are temporary adaptations of an individual and are *definitely not inherited* or passed on to the next generation.

The phenotype (physical characteristics) of the next generation individual are determined at birth by, and only by, the combination of genes that the individual received from his or her parents (genotype) at the time of conception. Now, in the case of a *population* (large number of individuals of a species), adaptation does have a genetic aspect. A *population* adapts to its environment by favoring those gene combinations within the species that produce individuals that are more adapted to their environment. This is like a special *breed* within a species. And this is a very important point: this group remains a breed **within the species, not a new species**.

The genotype (gene pool) of this breed is definitely skewed with a preponderance of gene combinations that produce the favored phenotype (physical characteristics) that is advantageous for surviving and thriving under these conditions. This is why St. Bernards and not Chihuahuas (both members of the species Canis – dog) are used for rescuing avalanche victims. Granted, dogs are bred "artificially" by humans to adapt them to special environments but they still remain dogs, and don't become a "new species".

This is observed naturally among different "breeds" of humans, who are all nevertheless human and not some other "species". Hence, aboriginal people who live in tropical areas generally have dark skin (high melanin for UV protection) and a higher surface area to volume ratio (tall and lanky - for easier heat dissipation). Conversely Inuits, the people of the Arctic regions, tend to have fair skin (low melanin – not much need for sun protection) but a considerably lower surface area to volume ratio (a propensity for portliness – for better heat retention).

So there certainly does seem to be a process in nature that also "breeds" species to adapt them to their environment. This is what Darwin called "natural selection". This is all still "adaptation" not "evolution". This natural process tends to "concentrate" certain gene combinations within the species that produce individuals that are more adapted to their environment. But these concentrations of certain genotypes within the gene pool of the species are just that: concentrations. When the conditions that favor this particular concentration of genes are removed, the concentration disperses and the "special breed" eventually ceases to exist, its genes becoming gradually diluted and dispersed throughout the vast general gene pool of their species at large. So far – so good. This is all solid science. But the next step is where Darwin's cart goes completely off its rails.

Darwin then made a leap of blind faith and this is where he, and all those who followed him, went off a cliff. Darwin *assumed* (he didn't observe – nobody has ever observed this) that these physical changes due to natural selection add up and ***eventually result in the formation of an entirely new species***. **This idea is called evolution**. This is where it crosses over from "adaptation", which is true science and which happens all the time, to "evolution", which is not true but a fantasy based on thin air and pure speculation and never happens in reality.

In all of these evolutionary philosophical fantasies there is not, nor has there ever been a single case, example, fact or even the slightest observation which might have supported them. The entire theory is meant to be swallowed as one whole, on blind faith, and subsequently never subjected to scrutiny or review. From the very start, evolution was presented by Huxley and Lyell as a seemingly well established fact beyond any doubt. This is drilled into every student in school to such a degree that the majority of people even to this day are incapable of doubting the veracity of this "fact", not to even mention researching it through genuine scientific methodology.

But many prominent scientists were very bewildered from the very start by such brazen forcefulness and the intrusion of philosophy and fables into the realm of science. The world press agencies unfailingly ignored or ridiculed these honest scientists. But when Mendel's discoveries in genetics finally became public, *even though this was forty years after their first publication*, it finally became necessary to subject the theory of evolution to scientific analysis.

In the beginning of the 20th century, it was finally understood that every species is primarily defined genetically (its DNA), not just morphologically (physical appearance), i.e., according to its *genotype*, and not only by its *phenotype*. Therefore, each species can only reproduce itself with the same species, and not any other. Attempts to interbreed with another species are always futile, because the DNA is incompatible, apart from a couple of exceptions. In such cases the offspring is left incapable of further reproduction. An example of such an offspring is a mule, which is the impotent offspring of a donkey and a horse.

At this point, the objective of the evolutionists became completely clear. In order to at least prove the *theoretical* possibility of evolution, it was necessary to produce, even by the most extreme artificial means, but nonetheless *produce* an organism which would continue to procreate among themselves, but would be reproductively incompatible (infertile) with its parent species.

With this aim, from the beginning of the 20th century, scientists began to breed a certain variety of fruit fly, called "Drosophila Melanogaster". This obliging little fly was capable of producing up to an amazing 25 generations a year. These poor fruit flies were subjected to every possible effect of radiation and all other types of extremes for over 800 generations. They were artificially mutated beyond recognition, resulting in extreme deformity. But each time, every offspring continued to breed freely with the previous generation (that is, with its parent species), except for cases when it was mutated to such an extreme deformity that virtually left it impotent. The experiment was fruitless, one could say.

It became apparent that it was impossible to exceed the boundaries of the genetic species. Contemporary attempts through "genetic engineering" to produce beings, which would interbreed amongst themselves, yet be incompatible with the previous, parent generation, are not only futile, but simply impossible.

The further science delved into the fable of "evolution", the more decisively all the inventions of this fantasy crumbled. Everywhere and at all times, the findings of science were actually the reverse and contrary to what evolution purported.

Paleontology (the study of fossils) for instance, having achieved quite a high level of competence in the gathering of remains, discovered, that not only did breeds and species not continuously change, as Darwin had hoped, but on the contrary, they all precisely differed one from another, and were always distinct and exactly the same as they exist today. Furthermore, all of them originated all at once, simultaneously, in completely perfect form and without any further changes in their species.

It was calculated that the number of every possible variation in the structure of only one DNA chain, could be counted up to the logarithm base 10 to the 87th degree! Of all of them, only one variation could be suitable to sustain life. Also, in each series of "amino bases", all must be *only* levorotory stereochemically, and not a single one can be dextrorotory, otherwise everything is disrupted. In other words, in this aspect blind chance is ruled out absolutely.

Regarding the practice of radiometric dating to establish age, science also refutes all suppositions regarding endless millions and billions of years. Radioactive carbon (C-14), for instance, is applicable only to the dating of organic material – bones and wood. Thus, since the half-life of C-14 is a little more than 5,000 years, its usage is then restricted to not more than a little over 3,000 years. And although this method is not completely accurate, stemming from the fact that many plants are equipped with a filtration system, which does not accept C-14, thereby significantly lowering the level of C-14 in animals which consume those plants, nonetheless the C-14 method for determining the age of the plant is based on quite a sound scientific foundation.

With regards to inorganic matter, i.e., rocks, one encounters contradictions which cast considerable doubt on the basic assumptions and occasionally even prove the exact opposite. All these methods *a priori* assume a constant rate of decay for all the radioactive isotopes in use today. There is no reason at all to assume that, especially in the face of evidence to the contrary, such as demonstrated by Dr. Robert Gentry.

One of the main methods for inorganic dating is based on the half-life decay of uranium into lead, which is (at the current rate of decay) four and one half billion years. The fact is that each time one individual atom of uranium degrades to lead, one atom of helium is released. Helium cannot react with anything and invariably moves upward, entirely accumulating on the surface of the atmosphere. In 1956 it was actually proven by Cook, a physical chemist and a Nobel prize candidate, that this helium cannot "exude" into space, as it had been presumed until then, because it cannot overcome the earth's gravity. If indeed the earth was as old as is supposed, based on the quantity of lead in rocks, which is presumed (without any grounds) to be all of radiogenic origin (that it all came from the decay of uranium), then there must certainly be a corresponding amount of helium in the atmosphere. In other words, in the atmosphere there must be at least one million times more helium than there actually is in which case all the air would be saturated with radiogenic helium.

In fact, the actual quantity of helium in the atmosphere corresponds at the utmost maximum to ten thousand years of degradation of all the earth's uranium. Not only that, but helium also enters into the atmosphere directly from the sun. It turns out that radioactive dating in actual fact demonstrates not the ancient age of earth, but its youthfulness, i.e., less than 10,000 years.

Archaeological digs have revealed that in certain cases, the deposits and sediments in cliffs are penetrated vertically by tree trunks. It is common among the evolutionists to believe that the formation of these deposits and layers took millions of years through the process of gradual dust settlement. If this were so, then of course it would be impossible for a tree to remain standing for millions of years while around it dust accumulated and gradually solidified into a cliff. Recently science clearly showed that the layers were formed very quickly, over the course of a few hours to a few days, via the process of "turbidity currents" which occur abundantly on the ocean floor. During this process, liquid mud flows along the bottom at a speed of more than 100 kilometers per hour, and having covered everything in its path, gradually petrifies.

Incidentally, the derivation of fossils can only be explained through this process: an organism being covered alive by mud, followed by a gradual replacement of its body by minerals contained in the water which swept the petrifying mud. In order to produce such an enormous quantity of fossils, a spontaneous elemental cataclysm must have occurred, on the scale of a world-wide flood.

This is not the venue to delve into a detailed scientific analysis of the fables of evolution, since already many brilliant scientific works have been written dealing specifically with this topic. But it is interesting to note that besides helium (or rather the lack of it), there are many other, purely scientific indications independent of one another, which indicate the relative youthfulness of the earth, that is, less than 10,000 years old. For instance, the amount of dust on the moon is apparently only around one centimeter, which corresponds to no more than 8,000 years of accumulation of space dust.

Another example – is the semi-degradation of the earth's magnetic field, which takes about 1,400 years. If one extrapolates this into the past, then one finds that already 10,000 years ago, the strength of the earth's magnetic field would have been 130 times stronger than at present. In order to produce a magnetic field of such power, the earth would have had to have its own nuclear source similar to the sun. Therefore, according to the disintegration of the earth's magnetic field, the age of the earth is again limited to less than 10,000 years.

The recent work of Robert Gentry very clearly demonstrates with even greater scientific subtlety that the solidification of the basic granite shields in the earth occurred very quickly, that is, in weeks, not in billions of years as the evolutionists think. Gentry did extensive work with "zircons" and with "radio-halos" in granite and likewise demonstrated very convincingly that the timeframe involved in the formation of geological columns was a matter of months, and not billions of years. Gentry also proved that the deposits of coal and oil could have occurred in a matter of weeks, under conditions such as those, which could have existed at the time of the Flood.

But despite all of this, science turned out to be powerless to prove the falseness of "evolution", because evolution is not a category within the realm of science, but of philosophy. Evolution did not proceed from science and does not contain anything scientific. Hence, science, with its methods, is simply not applicable to evolution. Evolution is accepted purely on faith, that evolution is a fact and therefore requires no further explanation. Those who believe in evolution presume that the factuality of evolution has long been completely proven, but no one seems to give any thought as to who did this, when and how?

Any question concerning the "factuality" of evolution, or a request for even the slightest substantiation or proof are immediately ridiculed and stifled as an absurdity not meriting a response. Many scientists with probing minds who doubt the "fact" of evolution, or simply do not believe in it, keep their thoughts to themselves because they value their careers. There are well known cases when a professor was dismissed from his position (for example, from the University of San Francisco) because he questioned certain premises in the *theory* of evolution.

Incidentally, evolution has even developed its own "dogma", the basic doctrines of which are beyond questioning. Essentially these doctrines contain the idea that matter and energy, sooner or later, under certain conditions, will spontaneously conceive, on their own, some form of elementary life. Life, once conceived, will also invariably and *without fail* begin the process of perfecting itself. Apparently there is no limit to this process of self-perfection, and the level of its perfection, or its *evolution*, depends primarily on time.

This idea had become so firmly entrenched in the consciousness and sub-consciousness of Western man, that by the end of the 19th century it was decisively the basic philosophy of

European and American societies, replacing the Christian outlook. The biblical account on the creation of the world and man, no longer were received literally, but as an allegory, or even simply as a myth.

In this way, evolution was already becoming not simply a philosophy, but was beginning to lay claim to the level of a new religion. Yet, the very idea of evolution was not quite so new. There is a known case involving a chief of a native Amazonian tribe, who listened with great interest to the sermon on Christ from Jesuit missionaries back in the beginning of the 20th century. He was already at the point of preparing to be baptized by them and have his entire tribe baptized, when he learned that the Jesuits believe in evolution. Then he was greatly disappointed and rejected Christianity, for it was evolution that had been his tribe's ancient religion and which he wished to be rid of. According to their native legend, their ancestors originated from monkeys, and when he learned that the Jesuits were teaching this also, he quickly expelled them.

Chapter Thirty Six —
The Spiritual Consequences of Evolutionism

However, Western intellectual society did not expel evolutionists, but rather elevated them to the most esteemed positions, as though they were the "priests" of the new cult of evolution. Scientists who did not embrace evolution were viewed as ignorant and were ostracized. Meanwhile, the evolutionists, on the contrary, were now referred to with the most honorary title of "scientists". Such scientists now occupied the foremost positions in society as the impartial, almost priest-like servants of the new truth, which would save mankind.

The Christian virtues of love, mercifulness, compassion, and meekness were forgotten, in general. They were replaced by the values of the new religion of evolutionism: the survival of the fittest. Now, survival and development at the expense of those less strong or capable in human society had not only ceased to be amoral and vile, on the contrary, became exemplary and even considered imperative for the good of common development and progress. This was what many persuaded themselves to believe, as for example, many of the industrialists of the late 19th and early 20th centuries, who built colossal fortunes for themselves, frequently with the grief and hardship of many of their fellow men.

The struggle for survival and individual prosperity extended further on to the struggle among the classes, and eventually the notion of "Social Darwinism" emerged. Karl Marx was thrilled by Darwin's writings and revered him to such a degree that he offered Darwin that he would dedicate his new book "Das Kapital" to him. But Darwin, with judicious tactfulness, declined such an honor.

The "fact" of evolution had gripped society to such an extent that even certain faithful Christians, not wishing to fall behind the progress of science, attempted to somehow reconcile the teaching of evolution with the teaching of the Church. They argued that God did create the world and even man through the evolutionary process. This was an extreme absurdity, proceeding from an incomplete understanding of either Divine Revelation, or evolution, or both. But it was namely this attempt to reconcile falsehood with truth, darkness with light, which was the very center of the spiritual danger of this "theory" of evolution.

Evolution fundamentally contradicts the Divine Revelation on the creation of the world. The fundamental contradiction boils down to the following: in essence, according to evolution, the world, and particularly life itself, gradually, constantly and invariably develops from lowest to highest, from simple to complex, from the primitive to the perfect. This expresses the conviction that that there is a constant, uninterrupted process, that is, everything, without fail, improves with time. The perfection, which will be achieved in another thousand years, will undoubtedly be superior to today's stage.

Such an extremely "positive" picture *completely excludes the notion of the fall*. It totally contradicts the teaching of Divine Revelation that God created the world and all forms of life, including man, whose *original* form was one of complete physical perfection, from which man fell. The Book of Genesis relates how man fell and nature, cursed by God on account of man, also fell and ever since has not been in a pattern of perfection, but degradation. Because of man's fall, *for the first time ever*, death had entered the world, not only for man but also for the entire animal world. And it was precisely because of the fall that man so crucially required the Saviour, without Whom man not only does not reach perfection, but perishes.

The coming of Christ the Saviour into the world was absolutely indispensable for the salvation of *fallen* man. Only Christ could abolish death and resurrect man at His second coming into the world, as He had already resurrected Himself previously. Only Christ can restore in man his lofty, original image and again give man the boundless possibility of perfecting himself in his God-likeness.

But according to evolution, there was never any fall, since there was never any aboriginal perfection. On the contrary, the animal world since its very primitive beginning, constantly is being perfected on its own and continues to develop to this very day, and will infinitely continue to be perfected. Therefore, according to evolution, there was no need for Christ to come and save man, since man has already been saving himself for a long time. Therefore, according to the contemporary outlook which is completely based on the evolutionary view, Christ does not offer us *salvation*, but rather at best, merely a moral teaching of peace and love which could certainly be beneficial for society and its further development, but not at all indispensable for the salvation of each individual person.

In this manner, even the slightest belief in the fable of evolution, fundamentally undermines genuine, Orthodox faith in Christ the Saviour. Contemporary society is so deeply infected by the ideology of evolution, having been raised on it from the cradle for five or six generations now, that the evolutionary outlook lies deeply imbedded in the subconscious of even a seemingly Orthodox believing Christian. Many believers even acknowledge that their faith in Christ has somehow been damaged, and has become somewhat intellectualized and they do not know how to acquire a genuine, simple "child-like" faith, the patristic Orthodox faith.

Besides this basic spiritual contradiction between evolution and Divine Revelation, there are other, more "technical" contradictions because of which it becomes impossible not only spiritually, but simply philosophically to adjust evolution to the teaching of the Church. Evolution is completely based on death. The survival of the fittest at the cost of the death of the weakest, and the transference of more adaptable traits to the next generation after the death of the previous generation, is the fundamental premise of evolution. Without death, evolution is not even conceivable. But the Church teaches, that in the aboriginal world, prior to man's fall, there was no death at all not only for man but even among animals.

Furthermore, the Church teaches, that God created the entire world, visible and invisible, out of *nothing*. Yet according to the theory of evolution, the world has always existed in one form or another. Even the basic axiom of contemporary evolutionary opinion, that matter and energy are not created nor are they destroyed, but exist infinitely, merely undergoing changes in form. According to this, the world is self-sufficient, and this falls precisely under the very first anathema of the Orthodox Church.

CHAPTER THIRTY SEVEN

Communism and Capitalism

By the end of the "romantic" 19th century, godlessness had fully ripened and consolidated itself in the "post-Christian" mindset. Having totally assimilated the moral precepts of evolutionism, society had gained a new direction for its further development, one based on socio-economic principles.

Any socio-economic system, as well as any political system for that matter, is only as good as the people in it. If everyone were a saint, or at least sincerely aspired to the Christian ideal of total love for God and love of one's neighbor as for oneself, then *any* socio-economic and political system would work perfectly well. In fact, then there would not be much need for socio-economic or political systems. If everyone only did onto others as they would have others do onto him or her, and if everyone looked out for the interests of others as much as they looked out for their own interests, then there would not be any need for laws at all.

This is actually the situation in the Kingdom of Christ that will ensue in the future age to come, after the Second coming of Christ and the dread Judgment of the world.Those who do their very best to attain to that calling to moral perfection that Christ has called everyone to, even though they may fall quite short, due to the fallen state of our human nature in this world now, nevertheless those who repent for their shortcomings and call on Christ for help, will be perfected by the Grace of God to be able to live in just such a world of moral perfection in the age to come. That world is what we call Heaven.

Until the appearance of. God in the world, humanity had wallowed in the depths of moral depravity for millennia. Even in the most civilized Rome, spectacles of lions devouring people and desperate gladiators mutilating and killing each other in front of large audiences in theaters was considered a very acceptable form of entertainment. Women were considered the property of men and could be treated as such. Newborn children who were not of the desired sex or physical qualities could be thrown off a cliff, as was the case with the Spartans. Human sacrifice to pagan gods, especially of virgins or infants was not uncommon and accepted among the pagan nations such as Aztecs and many others.

The coming of Jesus Christ into the world changed all that forever. His teaching was the leaven that made the bread of Heaven rise in the world. Cruelty and barbarism still do take place in the world, especially in societies not transformed by the Grace of Christ's teaching, but they are now regarded as atrocities and definitely unacceptable by world standards which are derived directly from the "Christianization" of society. As society "de-Christianizes" it also regresses morally and tends to return to the barbaric pre-Christian state. But the indelible mark of Christ's moral standard always remains, and still serves as the standard by which morality is judged.

Meanwhile, the world and humanity is in a fallen state. Generally, people are driven by greed and self-interest, often at the expense of their fellow man. The new ideology of evolutionism became manifested within the socio-economic sphere in two forms: the personal and social.

Capitalism

In its first form, the individual and his rights were deemed to be of the highest priority, as was the case with what came to be known as the "free world" in the 20th century and championed by America. This social structure granted the individual what it defined to be his or her "inalienable" rights to personal freedom and the pursuit of happiness (however defined by the individual), as long as this pursuit did not endanger or infringe on that same pursuit of other individuals in the society. This personal freedom of worship, of speech of assembly etc. is a natural, wonderful and God-given thing that many people sacrificed their lives to secure and it must never be taken for granted, because there is an unfortunate tendency in fallen human nature for people in power to oppress others who are not.

The pursuit of happiness generally came to be identified with the accumulation of personal wealth by whatever legal means possible. Thus the stage was set for an economic system that came to be known as "capitalism". The term "capitalism" stems from the Latin "capitale" which means "head", as in "capital city" or "capital idea', etc. In the economic sense, "capital" came to be known as a sum of money, invested by private individuals (capitalists) to launch a venture in the free enterprise system. Such a venture or enterprise would then operate in a market-driven economy where the basic economic laws of supply and demand, coupled with competition from similar enterprises determined the ultimate success or failure of each enterprise. Capital was the beginning and end (goal or purpose) of every enterprise and thus the system was called "capitalism".

Individuals, who wanted to launch an enterprise, or start a business of their own, but lacked sufficient capital to do so, could apply for loans from banks in order to do so. This naturally led to a proliferation of banks and other lending institutions that became the basic foundation of the mechanism of capitalism.

Technically, capitalism functions on the basis of credit. Entrepreneurs with marketable ideas can, in theory, obtain loans from banks (credits) which literally bring starting capital from non-existence into existence through nothing but the extension of credit, the sheer act of granting a loan. Most (up to ninety percent or sometimes much more) of this very money is not real but "virtual", i.e., in the form of a loan or "credit" to the bank account of the borrower. The new capital created through a bank loan then constitutes a debt of the borrower to the bank, which proceeds to earn daily interest for the bank until the loan is completely paid off. This interest, or compounded earnings, is what comprises the real income of the bank. When the loan is paid off, the bank crosses it out of its books and the initial capital influx ceases to exist, with only the interest on the loan, (the actual revenue) remaining.

As long as most people behave honestly and there is sufficient confidence, or faith in the system (no sudden panics or "runs on the bank") the whole system works like a well-oiled machine, based on reciprocal loans among banks, i.e. bank notes. At the top of this credit network in America stands the private, central bank known as the Federal Reserve. The Federal Reserve, even though it is a quasi-government private bank, issues base loans to all the banks within this system based on interest rates that it sets. Furthermore, this main bank has the sole right to independently set interest rates and to print currency which it launches into circulation, but again, only through a loan to the federal government known as a bond, which the government then sells.

This is not the appropriate venue to examine capitalism or communism in depth, since there are many thorough writings devoted to the subject that clearly interpret their ideas and mechanisms. However, they did emerge as the two competing socio-economic systems at the close of the nineteenth century and the struggle between them shaped much of the history in the twentieth century. For the purposes of this book, it is will suffice to provide a brief spiritual overview not only of capitalism, but of communism as well, to compare the two and to determine what makes them differ, in order to attempt to understand the spiritual ramifications of each and the affect that the struggle between them had on the Orthodox Church.

First, it is important to note that God *did* create man to be free and so God does not "force" anyone to conform. However, God *did* give man some very clear guidelines for behavior that is acceptable to Him and what is unacceptable. These are known as the Ten Commandments. These Ten Commandments were given as elementary guidelines of moral behavior to prepare man for the ultimate standard of moral perfection given to us by God when He came to us in the Person of Jesus Christ. This New Commandment that God has now given man is: "Love each other". This new standard of behavior is so lofty, so perfect that man cannot achieve it by only his own efforts without the essential assistance of God's Grace. This teaching of moral perfection, of total love, is promoted by the Church of Christ, which also provides us with the means to attain it — the fullness of Grace.

Capitalism essentially takes man as he is. It does not impose on man any ideology of how man is "supposed to be" and then force him to conform. It believes that everyone should be free to "live and let live". The French expression for this is "laissez-faire". Naturally, this unleashes boundless creativity and enterprise in individuals who are so inclined.

But here is where the paradox and the challenge of capitalism lies. While it encourages individuals to freely pursue each their own interest, it must, at the same time, keep those pursuits in check, to a necessary degree, so that they do not infringe on the interests of other individuals or on the interests of the state. Essentially, capitalism promotes and thrives on *egoism* but it must keep that egoism under some control by "external" means, that is to say, by a complicated system of laws and by-laws that it must vigilantly enforce. The problem is that trying to contain egoism in a net of legal structures is like trying to contain water in a very tight mesh. It will always find ways of leaking out.

This naturally leads to what can be called a "syndrome of perpetually sagging moral standards" in society. This is why things that are acceptable in one generation, were quite unacceptable in the previous generation, and yet in turn, will be considered prudish in the next. This is of course practically inevitable in a free society where the civil authority must operate on the slippery slope between personal freedoms and morality.

The point here is that effective control of immoral egoism can only be produced *internally* with each individual, not externally through law enforcement. Immoral behavior is a sin – a problem of the *will* of an individual and so, it can only be effectively dealt with in accordance with that same *will* of the individual. A person must *want* to be good, not be forced to be good. Laws can only do so much to restrain an individual with the will to circumvent them.

Returning once again to the analogy with water, morality in a free society will tend to keep seeping out and, like water, will tend to flow downstream until it "finds its own level". This "level" is naturally, the lowest common moral denominator in society and, as such, is not very healthy for society as a whole, nor salvific for individual members of it.

Fortunately, this inherent weakness of free society is also its strength. The freedom that it bestows on individuals and whose negative consequences it is then incapable of controlling in the long run strictly by legal means, that same freedom allows the Church to do *its* work in that field. This is the work of transforming individual members of the free society, one by one, from a fallen sinful condition to a life in Christ. This is not to say of course that every individual will be transformed from a sinner into a saint by the Church. But at least, and this is no small matter, the Church has the opportunity and each individual has the chance of it. And *this* is what makes all the difference in the world. And *this* is why "free" society, with "free" individuals, as God created them and as He intended them to be, *this* kind of society, by the Grace of God, prevails.

Communism

But communism, on the other hand, is doomed to fail from its very start, for it is based on a complete contradiction. Again, this is not the appropriate venue to delve into all the details of the theories of Marx and Engels, which are already far too well known to all. It is common knowledge that this is a socio-economic system which yields absolute priority to society at the cost of the individual. Hence, it is the extreme form of socialism, enforced by tyrannical dictatorship. Yet the contradiction of communism lies in the fact that it presents itself as a highly moral system, but in essence rejects the very foundation of morality – God Himself.

Where capitalism reinforces egoism, communism demands self-denial and sacrifice. Capitalism promotes effort as the means to achieve one's personal happiness for each person individually, thereby ensuring the overall health and strength of the nation. Communism prescribes effort (labor) for the sake of society, state and even the world's proletariat, since the only happiness of an idealistic communist is to liberate the proletariat of the entire world, which can only be achieved through a world-wide revolution. Communism seemingly preaches lofty idealism, but this is the idealism of atheism.

This would be the same as searching for the lightest possible hue within the darkest color of paint.

Communism, in its ideal distillation, tries to instill an extreme and distorted sense of social responsibility in each individual to the point that each individual is supposed to feel that they, as an individual, do not matter at all – only society matters. This kind of psychology may be natural for ant colonies but not for humans. Each human individual was made in the image of God and is completely unique and irreplaceable. We are taught by God to *"love your neighbor as yourself"*. Jesus Christ also taught us that no greater love has man than when he lays down his life for his neighbor. And this is precisely the point. This kind of self-sacrifice can only be done out of complete and perfect *love* for one's neighbor. And *this kind of love* can only be attained with abundant help of God's Grace.

The problem with communist ideology is that is unrealistic and unnatural. It expects and demands from individuals behavior and acts that can only be motivated by true and complete love for one's *neighbor*, that is people that we are in contact with, starting with our own family. But communism does not teach love for one's neighbor, and not even for one's family, but the ideal communist must be willing to sacrifice not only himself but also his family for the good of the "party". This was clearly illustrated when the Soviet government erected a monument to a young boy (Pavel Morozov) who betrayed his own parents to the communist authorities and who were then executed for being in disagreement with the communist authorities.

So, instead of love, communism tries to instill a fanatical devotion to the "cause of international revolution", to the communist "party" and in particular, to the leader of the party who is then promoted as a figure of worship, on par with a deity. This kind of devotion is not natural for people and, in the long run, nor really possible.

What "idealistic" communism tries to promote can only be accomplished by true and perfect love. But communism does not promote that kind of love. Instead of love, communism uses "brainwashing" propaganda and ultimately, force, to bring individuals into compliance with their objectives. This naturally promotes duplicity in the individuals. People learn to keep their true thoughts and feelings well to themselves and present an outward appearance only of what is expected of them by the "party". This creates a great gulf between appearance and reality in communist society.

Tragically, after several generations of people born and raised in this climate of total falseness, it seems that many, if not most, actually seem to lose the ability to differentiate between truth and falsity. People become so accustomed to *not* taking anything at face value, of *not* believing anybody, and of always finding ways to "beat the system" that they become virtually incapable of functioning in a "normal" society where "yes" is yes and "no" is no. Imagine someone who was born and lived every minute of their life in a house with very slanted floors, crooked ceilings and walls covered with highly distorting mirrors. This person would find it very difficult to adjust if placed suddenly in a "normal" house.

This is why communism was not capable of marching on without being supported from its very first step. Yet its promoters needed it to march on, and for its support idealistic slogans were immediately put into operation. But these slogans did not correspond at all to the reality at hand, and so, from its very beginning the entire system became completely bogged down in hypocrisy. This basic falsity of practical communism destined it to utter self-depletion from its very start. This falsity is the result of its central self-contradiction, for it calls for the denial of not only oneself, but even one's family, all for the sake of a higher common good. And yet, it simultaneously rejects the very source of all good – God. This is why the good which communism promotes is not "good" at all, but an illusion. And this is the lie that cannot be concealed.

CHAPTER THIRTY EIGHT

The First Half of the 20th Century

If the 19th century had finally affirmed godlessness through "science" and "philosophy", the 20th century bore the fruit of this godlessness. Among the first of such fruits was the Great War – the First "World" War for it saw the collapse of the entire institutional old world represented by the European monarchies and the social structure they embodied.

The main tragedy for the entire world was the removal of the Russian Orthodox Tsar, the last to restrain the onslaught of the evil of godlessness throughout the entire world. Holy Rus' crumbled from its summit into a deepest abyss.

We will not dwell on the reasons and process of the Russian revolution, for there are many marvelous works dedicated to this topic. But it must be noted that the overwhelming majority of Russian society, and particularly the intelligentsia had abandoned God, and had given itself over to passions and false teachings. Tolstoy, Blavatskaya, the sophists, theosophs, living church movement, etc., had taken control, enthralling society. Holy Saint John, the priest of Kronstadt, the Optina elders and many other of God's emissaries and prophets were avoided and ostracized.

But God will not be scorned. Had Russia not been endowed with the fullness of Grace and the True Church of God, it would not have been held to such a high accountability. But Russian society had for almost the previous 200 years increasingly disdained the Holiness of the Church of Christ, and finally got what it was askeing for. There is a saying that God is very patient, but will finally hit hard. Had Russia not betrayed Christ and His Church, Christ would not have handed Russia over into the hands of godless and pagan men. However, many of the godless men who overcame Russia were not its own at first, but international persons, well-organized and abundantly financed from abroad by people in whose interest it was to see Orthodox Russia destroyed.

The godless and cruel control over Russia was not the end objective of the revolution but merely one step. The final goal was, and continues to be, the further development of the mystery of iniquity mentioned in the Holy Scriptures, for which cause it was necessary to overcome the Russian Orthodox Church, if possible, in order to unite Her to global godlessness.

Even so, Russia was apparently not completely degenerate spiritually and yielded a tremendous host of new martyrs. They held the victory over satan with his false "church" and witnessed their loyalty to the Church of Christ by their glorious martyrdoms. Such an enormous feat can hardly remain fruitless. The blood of such a multitude of new martyrs, abundantly bedewed the Russian land and in due course will bring spiritual sobriety and the return of many to the Church of Christ – the One, Holy, Catholic and Apostolic.

After the Russian revolution, the mystery of iniquity now began to spread quickly throughout the entire world. The Second World War soon completed what the First had begun, and after it the world was now well pre-disposed to the building of a New World Order.

This is the point at which the drama of the conflict between communism and international capitalism began to develop, even though both systems had one common, final goal - the unification of the entire world under godless control.

The path of personal liberty and the opportunity for prosperity were applied in the West, and predominantly in America, in the pursuit of personal happiness. The American generation which had grown up in the squalor and deprivation of the Great Depression of the 1930's, later undergoing the horrors of WWII, returned home to a secure America. And many immigrants who reached the shores of America for the first time as a result of the perturbations of the war, for the first time acquired a real and almost limitless opportunity to finally have a well-established personal life, and most importantly, one for their children.

Europe was in shambles after WWII and in total need of all goods and services. America, which had not fought the war on its territory, was the only country to have a completely undamaged infrastructure, its institutions being completely untouched by the ravages of war. There was a colossal demand for everything and not only in all of Europe but in America as well. During that period America, essentially without any competition, obligingly and kind-heartedly took on the task of supplying the international market with all that it required.

Of course, this period saw no unemployment whatsoever, and all labor was well remunerated. Workers were promised that soon each would have his own house, a car in the garage and a turkey in the oven. The population was not at all spoiled, but experienced in patience and toil, and wholeheartedly embarked upon this task. Morale at the time was quite high among the American population, and the 1950's flowed by in an almost fairytale-like hue. The simplicity of morals and nearly childlike naiveté lent these years a certain aura of the American stereotype. America nostalgically recalls the years from 1942 to 1962 as the blessed time of carefree childhood. The population that had been exhausted by woes and war, was quite content to live a quiet life and make a decent life for themselves and their children. And there were many children born! From 1946 to 1962, to a significant degree, the largest generation ever in the history of America and Europe was born. This generation, a veritable harvest of infants became known as the "baby boomers".

Again, all was in place for drastic and monumental changes.

CHAPTER THIRTY NINE —
The 1960's

The generation of baby boomers grew up during quite extraordinary conditions in world history, as though in an incubator. All their needs were completely provided for, even with excess. In their blessed childhood no threats loomed over them except for the theoretical possibility of nuclear war. But in general the sky above their heads was virtually without a single gray cloud. They had been provided with everything except for that "one thing needful" - a spiritual life.

The boomers' parents had grown up in conditions of deprivation and war, which were so severe that not only did they have no opportunity to be educated in spiritual matters, but in many cases, they barely managed to obtain much formal education. But given the nearly total absence of spiritual knowledge, many of them still maintained a deep faith in God and respect for His church. Thus their children grew up in the 1950's, completely satiated with earthly food, but with a great lack of spiritual food. A unique generation developed, for it was the most numerous generation in history, and at the same time it experienced a great spiritual drought. In the beginning of the 1960's, America was the picture of material well-being and yet a spiritual desert.

The enemy of mankind did not bypass such a unique opportunity and selected a new weapon to pour out his "anti-grace" over the entire world. It is well known what a powerful effect music has on all living creatures and how profoundly it can influence people. He took advantage of the emerging "Rock" movement in popular music.

In 1964 four musicians arrived from England onto American soil, a new group with the strange name "Beatles". Although they lacked any formal musical education, they were naturally very talented, and possessed the ability to captivate human souls on an unprecedented scale. Prior to their arrival in America, they had played their guitars and drums in the pubs of Liverpool, and some parts of Europe without particular success. But after their first performance in America, the results were astounding.

Young girls, fifteen and sixteen years of age, squealed unnaturally, as though they were possessed, from the very beginning up to the very end of the concerts and often feinted. Although the first Beatles songs were quite simple and even silly, they managed to completely conquer the entire young generation in one fell swoop, starting with young girls who seemed to have been overcome by an irrepressible force similar to mass hypnosis.

The obsession with the Beatles was not limited to America and quickly spread across almost the entire world. The Beatles had taken control of the souls of adolescents to such a degree, that they were able to absolutely dictate to the youth not only fashion and tastes in all things, but even their basic views and attitudes toward everything.

Following the unbelievable success of the Beatles, America was flooded from England by an innumerable quantity of similar "musical" groups, among whom there were also overt Satanists. This phenomenon even entered into history under the title "the British Invasion".

Having conquered the younger generation within the space of two years, the Beatles left it under the control of many other generals from their invading "army" - a number of "rock stars". The Beatles themselves abruptly withdrew from the public view. There were two reasons why this sudden withdrawal was necessary. First reason was to take time for a concentrated preparation of the next phase of the conquest. The other reason was that after two years of unprecedented success, in 1966, the John Lennon (one of the Beatles) was quoted in the *San Francisco Chronicle* April 13, 1966 saying, "Christianity will go. It will vanish and shrink, I needn't argue about that; I'm right and I will be proven right. We're more popular than Jesus now".

This caused an enormous protest in America (unexpected even for the Beatles themselves), and they replied with some consternation that they had not intended to say that they are "better" than God, but simply that they are more popular than God Himself, adding, with disdain, if such a *thing* even exists. But such self-justification did not help them, and soon afterwards attacks against the Beatles began. Once, after their airplane landed, bullet holes were discovered in its wings and tail. And so, in 1966, after only two years, the Beatles decided to go into hiding for a while.

For almost two months, no one heard or saw anything of the Beatles. Many thought they might be finished altogether. But they were only just beginning. They worked intensely all that while, but only during the night, from evening till morning, in a clandestine studio in England. After almost eight months of this endeavor, the Beatles finally presented their new product to the world, an album entitled "Sergeant Pepper".

This record laid the foundation for the sub-culture of narcotics, psychodelia, and the so-called "anti-establishment" movement, or simply, "hippy" movement.

The Beatles now were leading the younger generation in a strange and new direction under the influence of LSD ("Lucy in the Sky with Diamonds"). The personal impression of the author is that narcotics, particularly LSD, chemically and physiologically open some access to certain parts of the brain, which after the fall of man, God closed to man. Possibly these would be such places where there could be heightened sensitivity to the surrounding spiritual world. But because our surrounding world is in a fallen state and therefore filled not with God's angels, but fallen spirits, such a ridiculous attempt to interact with spirits, or artificially delve into the fallen spiritual world is not only extremely harmful for man, but is even very dangerous. Sinful, fallen man, in taking such drugs without the protection of Grace, opens within himself access for fallen spirits and becomes the defenseless victim of their ghoulish illusions and destructive suggestions. This is a spiritual equivalent to a toddler wandering around in the jungle at night. Very often such drug induced "trips" ended in violent crime or suicide.

The "Beatles Revolution", as it became known, was now in full swing. The Beatles themselves returned to the world stage, but no longer in black suits with bowl-style haircuts. Now they appeared in psychedelic kaftans, sporting hair longer than most women. No longer would they sing silly verses for fifteen-year-old girls; they now challenged all of society to examine reality beyond the realm of human consciousness.

At this point, not only was everything now permissible, but even encouraged. The "sexual revolution" arrived and everyone was "liberated" of all former, out-dated precepts of morality and decency. "Free love" had arrived, and in general, all freedom from any responsibility. The youth (often in a drug-induced state) would preach peace and love to all, handing out flowers, especially to police constables and soldiers. Some people abandoned their work, schooling or families and congregated in order to live in "communes" or hostels, similar to camps where everything was communal.

In such situations there were common wives, husbands, and consequently children, and a common, abundant stash of narcotics. The youth worshiped the Beatles as their spiritual leaders and liberators, while the older generation recognized them a superb artists. The Queen of England even knighted them, after which certain English knights rejected their own knighthood in protest.

The gates were now wide open for everything and anything. Many things that previously had been even unthinkable in society, now became quite possible and could be pursued. The Beatles were prepared to go even farther. They traveled for a "retreat" to India, to prepare the third phase of their influence on world society, beginning in America.

CHAPTER FORTY —
Eastern Influence

The photograph of the Beatles, sitting at the feet of an eastern guru created an overwhelming impression on Western society. Suddenly India ceased to be the backward, spiritually ignorant country, but became the source of spiritual light and enlightenment for the entire world. The Beatles dove into Hinduism and scooped up a seemingly new, deep transcendental knowledge from it. Upon their return from India, they brought with them yoga, meditation, the notion of karma, mantras, and founded and disseminated a common belief in reincarnation. The Beatles were followed by innumerable Hindu "gurus" and teachers to feed the insatiable American appetite for Eastern exoticism.

Every person who was considered cultured, had not only his own psychiatrist, but now fashion required that he have a personal guru, under whose guidance a person could now spiritually develop. Many began to practice yoga, engage in meditation and read all the sources of eastern wisdom. It became extremely unpopular to call oneself a Christian.

Hinduism now flooded the spiritual desert of America and covered nearly everything. Hinduism is one of most ancient pagan religions personally founded by a demon with the name Krishna who essentially offers the very same teaching which he originally offered to Adam and Eve back in Paradise: *deification without the cross.* Hinduism preaches, in essence, the evolutionary process of deification, through a series of reincarnations to increasingly higher degrees, depending on the "karma" of a previous life. Such a teaching suddenly became not only clear and logical, for the evolutionary-minded Western man, but even somehow close to his heart. No cross, no Saviour – this was simply a natural process of gradual, spiritual perfection, reaching the ultimate goal – to be god. This ultimate point is called "Krishna consciousness" and is achieved by every person, sooner or later, when he finally realizes that he himself *is* god.

Following Hinduism, Buddhism seeped into the West. Buddhism became very popular among the educated and its influence deeply penetrated all of society through its various branches, such as Zen, for instance. Hinduism considers itself to be a universal and all-encompassing religion, containing within itself all the rest, even the Christian faith.

One of the main accomplishments which is attributed to the Beatles, is this if not complete unification of the world, then at least preparing the world for this unification. The Beatles gave the new generation a common language, common precepts, morals, goals, notwithstanding their geographic, economic or even political situations. They preached peace and love for the entire world. War began to be sharply condemned as something unnecessary, unwise and even the greatest evil. The great world movement of pacifism, the Peace Movement began. A sign consisting of two letters that stood for "nuclear disarmament" but looked like a broken cross was adopted as a symbol of this movement. The hero of that day, the Hindu Ghandi, became the greatest example of pacifistic resolution of conflict. Everyone pointed out the absurdity of the Viet Nam war where tens of thousands of young Americans were dying, as though all of it was in vain and pointless. They began to demand the immediate end of that shameful war.

The movement of universal disarmament began with a call to mutual world understanding. The world faced the terrifying threat of its complete annihilation through nuclear war. If the very possibility of a worldwide nuclear war was not perhaps quite so real as it was played up to be, in any case the *threat* of such a thing strongly motivated everyone toward the path of mutual understanding and resolution of conflicts by diplomatic means. The world embarked firmly onto the path of global concepts – a global economy, global politics instead of isolationism, and, of course, the path of a global religion.

Chapter Forty One —
The Development of Technology

It had been at the end of the 19th century when science attempted to swallow the idea of "evolution" and this idea of evolution became lodged like a bone in its throat. No longer being capable of discarding that theory due to "socio-economic" pressure, science began seemingly to choke on it, taking somewhat of a blow to its development. All future scientific developments would have to deal with "evolution", to either support it or draw conclusions from it. Taking into account that evolution is not a fact, but a pure figment of imagination, this circumstance greatly restricted the field of activity for science in the pursuit of truth.

Physics continued to develop, but along two strange, awkward and even divergent directions — Quantum Mechanics and Relativity. But the further it advanced, the more this development was built on suppositions which were also connected with the evolutionary world-view. Theories were increasingly built on assumptions, which in turn were built on other assumptions. Theoretical physics had directed itself into a practical dead end.

But although theoretical, or "pure" science had been seriously stricken by the illness of evolution, nonetheless, at the end of the 19th century, it brought technology into the world. In the late 19th and early 20th centuries, almost everything which we see in our modern world had been invented. Starting with quite primitive origins, technology began to develop and grow rapidly. Everything which Jules Verne had envisioned began to be produced and perfected.

In the whirlwind of technological development, life began to change quickly and the *tempo* of these changes began to overtake the capability of people to adapt to them. A certain syndrome emerged, known as "future shock", when people began to fall so behind the rapid changes in progress, that they could no longer manage to assimilate or absorb them, not to mention even incorporate them into their way of life. Because of that "future shock", as the sociologist Alvin Toffler described it, the majority of people lived not in their "real time", but always in the past. In any case, such a concept was forced on everyone, and people constantly lived in a pursuit of the latest technological advances, but never managing to keep pace with them and perpetually remained "behind".

In any case, many strongly felt that in their lives, a certain psychological "shift" or "dislocation" had occurred. This "shift" penetrated into all spheres of life and pervasively there was a sense of awkwardness and an "inorganic" sense of life. The spirit of those times was strongly reflected not only in science, but with even greater emphasis in music. There was a dissonance to music, a freakishness in art, and existentialism in literature. All of this reflected that "shift" and a certain sense of alienation and bewilderment that prevailed in the souls of people, on the backdrop of revolutions, wars throughout the world, and many drastic changes in their lifestyle because of the latest technological achievements.

Technology came to be identified with science, and to some degree, replaced science. The world now began to pay homage to that lofty concept of "high technology" and saw in it limitless possibilities for the improvement of its life as well as the primary means to resolve all its problems. During this time science fiction began to develop strongly and faith in it became so widespread and entrenched, that on occasion, in America, when a certain radio station by way of a prank aired a program on the invasion of the world by aliens from Mars, a large portion of the population was in such a state of terror, that some literally died from fear or killed themselves. This identical phenomenon of mass hysteria also occurred in Quito, Ecuador, on a separate occasion.

After those episodes, "Martians" began to visit the earth more frequently and often "flying saucers" would appear. The extraterrestrial alien cult began to develop quickly, firmly grounded on the hard foundation of evolution and inspired by a limitless popular faith in "highly evolved beings" with very "advanced technology".

Hardly anyone at the time questioned the value of such a surge in the development of technology and almost no one noticed its environmental impact or socially detrimental aspects. The world flung itself headlong into the open gates of "advanced technology" or "high tech" as it became known later and during that time no one could hesitate even if they wanted, to weigh the benefit versus its harm. Mankind found itself imprisoned by its technology and under its serious threat.

Life became completely different, with new demands and new dangers. In order to arrange and organize this new life in a beneficial manner, a new religion was required for the "New Age".

Chapter Forty Two —
The "New Age" Movement

The "New Age" movement had gradually begun to coalesce and take root at the end of the 1960's, during the reign of the Beatles. The spirit of the "New Age" began to permeate literally all aspects of life and became evident in many various and distinct sectors. But the sectors affected by the spirit of the "New Age", although separate and independent, all began to freely intertwine into loosely formed "networks". In turn, these networks began to freely merge into "webs" and then "megawebs". From diet to politics, from ecology to gymnastics, from art to philosophy and religion – everything began to interconnect spontaneously on the grounds of some sort of new spirituality.

Essentially, this spirituality was ancient, pagan Hinduism that began to strongly embed itself in the West after the impact created by the Beatles. But this had become a new and transformed Hinduism, distinct from the ancient "classical" Hinduism that abjectly rejected the world, calling everything material an illusion (*Maya* in Hindi), which was merely an obstacle for the spiritual world which, according to classical Hinduism, was the only reality.

The new Hinduism on which the "New Age" movement is based, had a far more positive view of the material world. It asserted the value of nature, man, culture, science, and even technology. The adherents to the "New Age" movement welcomed technological developments and all the resulting complications in life as long as they follow the path of global peace, global unification and ecological balance. In essence, the "New Age" movement is based on pagan pantheism, which combines all things spiritual and material into one, and therefore, the basic, common faith of all "New Age" adherents is that everything is one. *Everything is one and everything is god.* This is the main motto of the New Age teaching, which unites all apparently separate and seemingly diverse movements and teachings comprising the all-encompassing "New Age" movement.

But the "New Age" is not merely Hinduism which has been refashioned into a Western style form. Nor is it simply a cult, even though it contains numerous and various cults. The "New Age" is the dawn of a real, new, global religion. This new religion is very eclectic, hence the new-agers typically glean what, in their opinion, is best from many sources, starting with astrology and shamanism, up to Christianity and even Orthodoxy.

The spiritual power for their mysticism, which permeates all of its aspects, is abundantly provided not by the Holy Spirit, but by a fallen spirit. The result is a colorful mosaic of all possible beliefs, traditions, philosophies – in a word, total and all-encompassing gnosticism. From Egyptian pyramids and crystals to numerology and the kabbala; from theosophy and scientology to transcendental meditation; all of this is thrown into one kettle and is cooked together. This organic "wholeness" is the primary characteristic of the "new age" movement.

The main criterion for incorporating something into the "New Age" teaching is simply the subjective judgment of each individual new-ager and is based solely on his own personal "experience". The new-agers do not accept any objective, spiritual truth and therefore disdain any "dogma" or any teaching concerning objective facts. Many of them supposedly believe in the divinity of Jesus Christ, but are quick to emphasize that this very divinity is natural for *every* person, and Jesus Christ merely showed an example of it.

In its most concise form, the belief of the "new age" movement consists of the following:

1. God is everything and everything is God.

2. Individual and personal "enlightenment" is vital for every person, because people live in a sinful state of ignorance that every individual is himself god.

3. An altered state of consciousness, contact with spirits and manifestations of supernatural psychic powers are all paths to achieving this consciousness (realization), i.e., that every person is god himself. The more the person becomes aware that he himself is god, the more he "realizes" his enormous potential and becomes endowed with abilities and supreme powers.

4. It is necessary to "expand the network" throughout the entire world, which means to organize people of like mind in order to achieve *one* world, with one global, political, social structure, with one economy and one religion.

It is a known fact that the most successful marketing result is achieved when the market is supplied with exactly those goods it demands, and not with goods which are forced on it. The enemy of mankind understood this perfectly long ago, and always supplied man with precisely those "products" to which man is most pre-disposed, and therefore most apt to receive. For instance, in the days of ancient Greece, when the Greeks prized physical perfection above all and worshipped their hero-warriors and the beauty of women, the demons supplied the Greeks with such gods that personified precisely those qualities. The ancient Greeks not only perceived their god-demons in the form of exquisite women and men, at times, apparently they even had physical relations with them.

And likewise, in the middle ages, when people superstitiously believed in witches flying on brooms, the demons again were happy to oblige and endeavored to show them many such spectacles.

In the end of the 20th century, when people were literally on the verge of worshiping "high technology", the same demons began with pleasure to show them examples of science fiction "technology", the demons' UFO's. Everything is given to a man according to his faith. People began to believe in alien visits to earth to such a degree that often they were vouchsafed not only to see them, but even, on occasion to be personally visited by them and have contact with them. However, after every such contact with "extraterrestrial beings", the victims were left in a profoundly disturbed psychological state and some simply would commit suicide. But these "sightings", although quite numerous, always remained purely "mystical" without any real and tangible proof.

Yet, the belief in highly-evolved alien beings with their highly advanced technologies, even "mystical" technologies, only grew and spread to such a degree that by the end of the 20th century, enormous private and even federal resources were applied to programs with the purpose of finding alien life, or at least to enter into communications with it.

But the "alien beings" not only took pleasure by appearing and mocking the human race, but in certain cases, in personal contacts with select few, they even preached their "supreme wisdom", like the oracles of ancient pagan Greece. And what an interesting coincidence... the preaching of these aliens precisely revolved around the imperative need for people of the entire world to unite. The reason for this absolutely essential need to unite was that the technology of humans had advanced to the point that it threatened to wipe out the entire world. In other words, man's technology had overtaken man's spiritual development to such a degree, that in order to survive and properly make use of their technology (*appropriate technology* – New Age expression), people must be "transformed" spiritually. But for such a global "transformation", it was necessary to discard all the outdated, backward and even dangerous causes of division among mankind. This primarily includes the differences among religions with their endless internecine strife, followed by racial prejudices, political conflicts, etc. In a word, the world must totally unite; for if it does not, it will certainly come to an end, self-destruct actually.

And so, in the new age, everything is being joined together into one. Science, for instance is merging with religion. According to the program of evolution, mankind now stands on the threshold of the next evolutionary step, by which it will move to the next, higher step – the spiritualization of its material nature. Science has long been involved in studying all sorts of occult and paranormal phenomena of this natural "spirituality".

In the pantheism of the new age, ecology too is merging with the pagan worship of "mother nature", and specifically "mother earth". Instead of respecting nature as a creation of God, and treating it with care, as God had commanded Adam still in Paradise, in the spirit of the "New Age" there is a strongly increasing tendency to deify nature and to respect it not as a creation of God, but as a divinity in and of itself. Much of the obvious design in nature is now common to attribute to "Mother Nature" instead of to God, the Father as it should be.

But the main spiritual danger, particularly for members of the Orthodox Church, is the irrepressible tendency to unite all religions and all churches. The spirit of the times is so strong, that in the 20th century, like never before, many of the great and bright stars of the ancient Orthodox Churches, which had "rightly divided the word of the Truth" for almost 2,000 years, have begun to fall from the sky.

CHAPTER FORTY THREE —
The Orthodox Church

Every epoch in the two thousand year history of the Church has had its particular heresies to deal with. The Church of Christ, as a unique and living organism, has always managed to keep itself separate from all the heretical groups that distorted the teaching and the living tradition of the Church, as it was passed down undistorted from the apostles of Christ.

The main heresies of our age revolve around the essence of the Church itself. There is a great deal of confusion now as to where *is* the Church. Where are Her boundaries and how do we know if we are in the Church or not. Some people even say that they do not believe in "organized religion". That all depends on *who* organized the religion.

If the religion in question was organized only by a person or persons, then it is certainly not worth believing in. But the religion that was organized by God Himself, Jesus Christ, is certainly worth believing in. Jesus Christ is the only one who has the right to "organize" a religion because He is God Himself and creator of all. This fact He proved beyond any possible doubt by actually resurrecting from the dead, exactly as He had predicted.

It's important, however, to keep in mind that Jesus Christ did not found "Christianity".

Jesus said, "I will build my Church and the gates of hell will not prevail against it" (Mat 16:18). What Jesus built was, and to this day remains, is the Church. The word "Christian" did not even begin to be used until more than a century later. One was, and still is, either a member of the Church or not. There were no "Christians" outside the actual Church that Christ built by the Holy Spirit through His apostles.

To become a member of the Church one had to (and still does) undergo a specific process, as established by the apostles. The process is somewhat akin to becoming a citizen of a country of the world, except that there is in addition a spiritual dimension to the process, through triple immersion in water in the Name of The Holy Trinity, and then the apostolic laying on of hands, or chrismation, that changes forever the spiritual reality for the new member.

If someone wishes to become an American, for example, they need to go through a procedure to finally arrive at the point where they are "made" an American by someone who is authorized and empowered by America to do so. After that point, the new American is in fact an American. This person was *not* an American until he or she was actually *made* into an American by someone authorized to do so, regardless of whether he believed as an American does, whether he considered himself to be an American or even if someone else (not authorized by the INS of America) proclaimed them to be an American.

Similarly, when a person becomes a member of the Church, he or she becomes a citizen, as it were, of the kingdom of Christ. This person also does not just decide to be a "Christian" and thus automatically become a member of the Church. This person also first becomes a "catechumen" (one who is undergoing instruction) and then, when he or she is ready, they are made a member of the Church by a person authorized to do so by the apostles. This authorized person is either a bishop of direct apostolic succession or a priest ordained by such a bishop.

Naturally, this new member of the Church, just as a new citizen, acquires immense privileges (the real possibility of eternal live, for a start) and also certain responsibilities, as is the case with any citizenship. The new member actually renounces allegiance to the prince of this world (Satan) and gives allegiance to Jesus Christ, the Son of God. They are now expected to abide by the laws and rules established by Christ and his apostles as guided by the Holy Spirit.

The faithful members of the Church eat the real flesh and drink the real blood of Jesus Christ (in the appearance of bread and wine) in the holy mystery of Communion and thereby actually *become* the mystical Body of Christ. This unites all the members of the Church into One, Holy and indivisible living body of Christ, known as the Church of Christ. This is clearly a separate living organism, which cannot accept any extraneous teachings or beliefs. The spiritual conscience of the Church has always acted as a sort of autoimmune mechanism to identify and expel any teaching and practice that is alien to the Church.

Doctrine that did not come from the Holy Spirit and through the Apostles in the Church is considered as poison and is absolutely not permitted to enter into the teaching of the Church. Such a foreign doctrine would serve to "mutate" the "spiritual DNA", or the dogma, of the living organism of the Church. Such mutations would cause distortion in the purity of the Apostolic Faith and lead to deformities in the practice of the Faith. This, in turn would bring about a great risk of spiritual death to those members who accept this false teaching.

For this reason the Church, as any living organism, tries to bring back to spiritual health any member that has been infected by a false teaching or heresy. The Church does this only by teaching the true apostolic, or Orthodox Faith to the ailing member and by trying to show the falseness of the teaching that they are being misled by. If the member does not respond and persists in the false teaching, and especially, if they begin to spread the false teaching, thereby infecting and distorting the faith of other members, then the Church must, according to the words of Jesus Christ, separate that member or members from its body to protect and preserve the other members from the spiritual disease of the false teaching.

As a physical body must amputate a sick member that cannot be healed, so the body of the Church anathematizes a member who persists in a heresy. This is done solely out of love for God and His Truth and out of love and concern not only for the healthy members of the Church but also for the ailing members themselves, in a last ditch effort to bring them to a sober understanding of the false path they are on and the spiritually grave consequences of it.

It is important to understand that the anathema that the Church pronounces on a false teaching and on those who hold that false teaching, the anathema is not an expression of hatred or malice or even "intolerance" to an individual per se. On the contrary, as noted above, it is an expression of love and concern for the purity and Truth of the Church's apostolic teaching, love and concern for the Church's members and even the individual in heresy. The "intolerance" is to the false teaching and not to the individual afflicted by it.

This is all because the dogma of the Church is a sacred, pure and holy teaching that has been revealed to humans by God Himself through the apostles at the descent of the Holy Spirit at Pentecost. This revealed teaching is complete, eternal and unchanging for all time. It is *not* the subjective understandings of individuals or something that humans "figured out", nor is it a matter of opinion. It is entirely objective fact revealed to mankind by God the Father through Jesus Christ and then fulfilled by the Holy Spirit in the apostles. For this reason the Church has always drawn a very clear line between this pure, revealed, in a word - Orthodox teaching and all the false teachings, conjured up by individuals.

The actual meaning of the term "Orthodox" is "correct belief". It comes from the Greek "ortho" which means "right" or "true" or "correct" and from the Greek word "doxa", which originally meant "common belief" and then also began to mean "glory" after the Hebrew word "kavod", which meant "glory" was translated as "doxa" in the Septuagint in the third century BC.

The Orthodox Church is that original, apostolic Church of Christ. It contains the entire fullness of God's revelation to mankind, along with everything that is necessary for man's eternal salvation. As was already stated, this revelation is of Divine origin, not of human origin. This is why humans cannot and must not alter in any way the content of this revealed Truth, known as the dogmas of the Church. Any attempt to add to the fullness of revelation or to take away from it, only serves to distort it. This is why the Orthodox Church has never accepted any "new" teaching or any new "developments" in theology that were not of apostolic origin.

Many of the external forms of tradition were developed over time by the local (orthodox) churches, which were in accordance with the pious traditions of the Church and suited the local cultural and ethnic traditions. But the actual dogmas of the Church, as stated in the Orthodox Creed, have always remained and will always remain constant for all time.

The real and genuine Church of Christ is that Church, which has continuous, unbroken apostolic succession or lineage, and which holds and teaches all the original dogmas of the apostolic teaching unaltered, and which has not accepted any false teachings or heresies, and which has remained absolutely faithful to Christ not only in word but also in spirit and deed. This is the Church that is full of Grace and in which the Holy Spirit lives and protects and guides Her as He did from the beginning.

There is very little of this Church left in the world now, even among the churches that call themselves "orthodox". But this Church remains, and according to the promise of Christ will remain right up to the Second Coming of Christ and the Great Judgment.

CHAPTER FORTY FOUR —
Ecumenism

The heresy that most afflicted the Church in the 20th and now, the 21st century is what is rightly called the "heresy of heresies" – Ecumenism.

Ecumenism is generally defined and understood to be a movement whose aim is to bring unity to Christian Churches separated by doctrine and practice and to Christian communities and generally, to believers in Christ. The underlying idea is that there should be a single Christian Church. Clearly, this is based on the belief that the Church of Christ is no longer One but it has split up into many churches, separated by doctrine and practice.

The problem with this view, and this is what actually makes Ecumenism a heresy, is that it denies the very dogma, the very essence that the Church is defined by: Unity. The Ecumenist platform presupposes that there is not One Church of Christ now but several.

As has already been mentioned previously, the Church was defined from the very beginning primarily as One, then as Holy, then Catholic (meaning Universal) and finally, as Apostolic. This is not mere wishful thinking, but an actual fact that is inseparable from the very nature of the Church. The Body of Christ is indivisible, indestructible and eternal. The Church can be persecuted and oppressed but it cannot be divided or altered (by heresy) or destroyed. As the resurrected body of

Christ is pure, whole and eternal, so exactly is His mystical Body. His Church is pure, whole and eternal.

The problem with Ecumenism is that it is based on erroneous understanding of what the dogmas of the Church really are. As was stated above, these dogmas are eternal Truth, revealed to us, humans, by the Holy Spirit, through the apostles of Christ. These dogmas are not ours to negotiate with, to alter and bargain with. It is not ours to bargain with the pure dogmas of the Church and to reach some sort of compromises with them. They were given to us as complete, holy and unalterable for all time. Ours is to keep them such and to abide by them, never to alter them or compromise them.

And this is exactly the point. Ecumenism, as defined and practiced today, attempts to find and reach *compromises* between all the doctrines. Ecumenists generally do not expect anyone to simply drop all the differing beliefs and views that had separated them from other "denominations" over the span of centuries.

Instead of trying to find the genuine, true, original, apostolic doctrine or belief, ecumenists try to find "common ground" among the various doctrines and beliefs and heresies. This is done with a view to establish commonality in some fundamental issues and then try to reach compromises with all the rest in order to bring about a sort of "deal". The point here is that the symbol of the followers of Christ is the Cross, not a negotiating table.

There is a notion that the divisions and separations among the "Churches" are caused merely by human factors, such as obstinacy or ego and that, despite these "superficial" splits, there nevertheless exists a "mystical" Church that is above and beyond these petty human discords. This notion is dead wrong. There has never been any such teaching in the history of the Church. Jesus Christ prayed to His Father that His Church be One, just as inseparable and indivisible as The Holy Trinity. Christ taught that anyone who does not listen to the Church and sows discord must be regarded as a heathen and *not* a member of His Church.

Contemporary ecumenism had its inception back in the late 19th century, during the era of the very height of universal "scientific" godlessness. It was then, in 1892, that in Chicago the world conference of leaders of all world "churches" took place. This conference (which was not exactly holy), was addressed by the 33-year-old Persian Archbishop of the Nestorian Church, a certain John Joseph, prince of Noisk. This bishop's report dealt with his recent personal trip to Mt. Ararat with the purpose of visiting Noah's Ark.

Not long before this, God had again revealed the Ark through a great earthquake on the night of the 20th of June, 1840, when more than seven cubic miles of Mt. Ararat collapsed and buried the villages at the foot of the mountain, including an ancient vineyard which, according to local tradition, had been planted by Noah himself. The Ark had been concealed by God through a previous earthquake in the year 400, when an army from the east was moving toward the Ark with the purpose of destroying it. At the time, the earthquake destroyed this army and hid the Ark between boulders and under ice, where it remained for 1440 years, until the year 1840.

In 1840, on the very eve of the proclamation of evolution, God again revealed the Ark to the world, perhaps in order to bring people to their senses, and to safeguard them from false and harmful teachings.

Archbishop John measured the Ark and recorded its length as being approximately 500 feet (160 meters) and counted more than 300 rooms and large cages within it, many with metal bars. When he revealed his findings to the conference in Chicago, he was laughed to scorn and his report was even stricken from the minutes of the meeting as something absurd and comical.

This was reminiscent of the appearance of Christ in Dostoevsky's "Grand Inquisitor" because the re-appearance of the Ark in 1892 was quite contrary to the purposes of the World Council of Churches. Far from wishing to be enlightened by facts, they had a completely different agenda. They needed to launch preparatory work for the ultimate unification of all world churches.

Orthodox Christians have always believed, and will always believe, in the absolute and indivisible unity of the One Church. This is how the Church Herself has defined Herself, from Her very beginning, thus introducing into Her unchangeable Creed: "I believe in One, Holy, Catholic and Apostolic Church." The movement of ecumenism is one of the principal components of the overall "New Age" movement. Thus, ecumenism holds as its goal the unification of all churches and the *creation* of One World Church. Thereby, ecumenism refutes that the One Church *already* exists, and has existed uninterruptedly from Her very beginning, on the day the Holy Spirit descended on the Apostles.

Ecumenism is the most pernicious and obvious heresy. Colossal efforts are required in order to integrate it into the various churches. Therefore, the preparatory work was conducted very carefully and diligently over the course of the entire 20th century. Gradually, the Orthodox Churches began to "modernize", to adopt the "new calendar", to abolish fasts, shorten services, and in general, in all spiritual, moral and ethical aspects, became ever increasingly more "liberal". This was necessary in order to bring them closer in line with the Western churches, which had already gone far off along the path of liberalization.

This work, of course, is always conducted from the top, from the hierarchical level, and not from the bottom i.e., the pious people. The enemy assumes that if he can gain control over the episcopate, then he will gain control of the entire Church, because the Church is *Apostolic*, hence, there is no Church without a Bishop, for where the Bishop is, there is the Church.

This is why, particularly in the 20th century, many "wolves in sheep's clothing" appeared, who led a multitude of Orthodox people into perdition. Consequently, when a bishop ceases to be Orthodox, that is, he ceases to "rightly divide the Word of Christ's Truth", the personal responsibility falls on each member of the Church within the jurisdiction of that bishop, to leave that bishop and go under the omophorion of an Orthodox bishop. Otherwise, if a person does not leave such a bishop who has fallen into heresy and remains under him, he will no longer be under the rule of Christ, but under the rule of the enemy of Christ who has taken command of such a bishop. Even if one's parish priest (batiushka) is a right-believing and pious clergyman, a person can find himself outside the Church if his bishop has left the Church and led his flock astray behind him.

To leave one's bishop and go under the omophorion of another is a very extreme measure and must be resorted to only in the most extreme cases and unavoidable circumstances. To judge any man, particularly a bishop, for personal sins and misdeeds is very sinful and strictly forbidden by the Church. But when a bishop distorts Orthodox teaching or introduces an obvious heresy, an Orthodox person is *obligated* to depart from him for the sake of one's own salvation.

It is extremely dangerous and inadvisable for any individual, especially if they are not highly knowledgeable and experienced in Orthodox theology, to judge, on their own accord, whether a bishop's teaching is Orthodox or not. And in almost all cases such conduct must be severely reprimanded. But there are cases, when a bishop is proclaiming, teaching or practicing a heresy, already condemned by the Orthodox Church as a heresy, albeit at a local council, when such a grave decision on the part of an Orthodox Christian is not only permissible, but obligatory.

Such is the case, for instance with the heresy of Ecumenism, which was condemned by the Russian Orthodox Church Abroad. The anathema for Ecumenism, as well as for all the other heresies anathematized by the orthodox Church over its two-thousand year history, is re-iterated at hierarchical services during the rite of "The Triumph of Orthodoxy" on the first Sunday of Great Lent.

Nonetheless, the preparatory work for the unification of churches was conducted by fallen and corrupted bishops throughout the 20th century, but very gradually, because the faithful laity had always resisted. In order to avoid disturbing the flock, this work was always conducted secretly within the highest circles following the example of Pharisees. The leaders of many world religions have long considered themselves to be "as one", regardless of doctrinal differences or heresies, but avoided public displays of their unity until the people would be sufficiently prepared.

With regard to religions that do not believe in Jesus Christ as the Son of God, it is essential to keep clearly in mind that Jesus taught *"I am the Way, and the Truth, and the Life. No one comes to the Father except through me"*. (John 14:6) And Apostle John wrote in his first epistle "Whosoever denies the Son does not have the Father, the one who confesses the Son has the Father also" (1 John 2: 23.)

The spirit of the "New Age", with its irrepressible striving to unite one and all, sooner or later, if God so allows, will create something akin to a unified world "church". This church may perhaps be "one" politically or administratively, but never One in the Spirit of Truth, the Holy Spirit. And this new world church will in no way be the Apostolic Church, for it will not be filled with the Holy Spirit through Apostolic succession nor will it abide by the Apostolic teachings and Apostolic cannons. The spirit in it will be far from holy, and therefore, that church also will be far from holy.

CHAPTER FORTY FIVE —
The Spiritual Delusion of the anti-Christ

The mystery of iniquity has been long at work in the world and the spirit of the anti-Christ continues to grow stronger. Wherein does this spirit of the anti-Christ lie? In one word – it lies in "prelest" (spiritual delusion). Prelest is a spiritual counterfeit. Every person unfortunately is afflicted by prelest, to a greater or lesser degree.

Most of us humans, in our fallen condition, tend to live between spiritual apathy and indifference on the one hand, and spiritual conceit and delusion on the other.

It is only with much sustained and prolonged effort and with much help from God that we begin to acquire that spiritual sobriety that allows us to see spiritual phenomena for what they really are.

The anti-Christ will not be a clear and open enemy of Christ, by no means! He will imitate Christ in all ways, in order to convince people that he is Christ Himself. His moniker is derived from the prefix "anti", which means "instead of"; and "Christ", which means God's Anointed One, or Messiah. In appearance, he will be kind, gentle, patient and merciful. He will attract everyone by his "love" and will amaze everyone with his "miracles" but this "love" will be false just as the "miracles" will likewise be false.

Moreover, this "love" will not be salvific for the people, but destructive because it will not call people to genuine repentance, to take up one's Cross, to spiritual rebirth through the Holy Spirit in the True Church of Christ – the Orthodox Church. No, the anti-Christ's love will condone human passions.

From the very beginning, in Paradise, when man fell, he did not want to hear about his sin; he did not wish to repent and be forgiven. He wanted to remain in his sin and justify it. The anti-Christ will not rebuke passions and call people to genuine contrition of heart in order to forgive and heal them, but on the contrary will justify them just as they are. It will make people feel good about themselves as they are.

Christ offers us salvation through faith in Jesus Christ, repentance, through each person bearing his own cross, in other words, through the humbling of one's pride, obedience to God, and through God's Grace. The anti-Christ, the one who is instead of Christ, offers man false "salvation" but only through self-justification, through sustaining one's pride, vanity and through the false anti-Christ "grace" - prelest.

It will only be in the last period of time given to the anti-Christ, that he will begin to forcefully and openly persecute the small remnant that will be left from the Church of Christ. Prior to that he himself will be as a church leader, very likely dressed in vestments and a mitre. At first he will protect and develop the "church". He will build temples, open them, bless them, etc. He will love everyone, have mercy on all and forgive all, particularly all heresies and superstitions. He will be filled with "anti-Grace" - a strong but false spiritual charisma, and all those who have become accustomed to mistaking prelest for true Grace will gravitate toward him.

What is the meaning of prelest? Again, it is a forgery, a false spirituality, an imitation of genuine holy spirituality. Prelest is always based on spiritual pride or spiritual conceit, or at least, satisfaction with one's spiritual state – on spiritual smugness. The more refined the spiritual pride, the stronger the prelest.

The problem with prelest is that a person who is in prelest is incapable of discerning that he is in prelest, and is incapable of emerging from it, as though he is stuck in quagmire. Even all attempts to dissuade him from his prelest can only engulf him deeper in it. The best means for healing from prelest is increased prayer and fasting offered by other people for the person suffering from prelest.

It is even better, in general, to avoid prelest and try not to succumb to it. This, of course, is very difficult because all people are afflicted most of all by pride and vanity and are very adept at persuading themselves of things they desire. This is precisely what the enemy uses. He very capably and closely studies a man's passions and the yearnings of his heart. Then he quite unnoticeably and gradually provides man with an opportunity to show his "spirituality" and then awards him with his own (demonic) "spiritual fruits".

To safeguard oneself against prelest, one must constantly *sincerely* sense in one's heart one's extreme sinfulness and, consequently, one's complete unworthiness before God and before every man. But our sinfulness, for the most part, is hidden from us, lest we fall into despair. Therefore we implore God in prayer, to grant us to "see our transgressions", in order to come to contrition of heart over them, and with the help of Grace, to struggle against them.

Traditionally in the Church, one of the most effective defenses against prelest has been spiritual obedience to a holy, wise and experienced elder, or spiritual guide endowed with a special Grace from God for guiding others. In the absence of such an elder, the next best safeguard is counsel with other pious and trusted members of the church and in particular pious and discerning bishops or priests.

In addition, it is essential to read and study and *assimilate* traditional patristic writings in order to acquire that patristic and Orthodox frame of mind. If we manage to acquire to some degree that state of mind, then we can much more clearly see our way, the Orthodox way, through all the mires and obstacles that the enemy of our salvation strews in our path.

The battle with anti-Christ is not political, nor economic, and of course not technological but rather, *spiritual*. The battle with anti-Christ is primarily the battle with one's own passions, or euphemistically speaking, with one's "weaknesses". A passion is a spiritually "rotten" place in our hearts, which rots because of the sins deeply rooted therein.

A sin becomes a passion through repetition and by our becoming accustomed to it, almost like a second nature. If a man is unaccustomed to struggling with his passions, then the enemy, like a predator, knowing well the "soft spot" in the man's heart, sinks his hook into that spot. A man who is unaccustomed to turning to God's Grace for help in the struggle against his own passions, does not want, or is no longer capable of rejecting that passion or weakness; such a man is not prepared to rip it out of his heart. And so, when the enemy tugs at the hook, he reels in the entire man.

Even if a man had struggled and even if he had been successful in the battle against his many passions, yet if he reserved for himself one secret passion which he nurtured, then he is in great danger of being caught through that one passion. All persons have their own passions ranging from the most base carnal passions to the most subtle spiritual pride. But all of them are capable of easily destroying a man. When a man stumbles on his passion, like into a trap, he can find himself incapable of cutting it off from himself, and the enemy begins to reel him in. Woe to the man in that situation if instead of repentance and a plea for spiritual help, he begins to justify himself. This is a terrible moment in the life of a man, when in one instant, he could lose all his spiritual dignity and even eternal life.

Such a man, if he succumbs at that moment, then begins to convince himself that he acted appropriately. Having persuaded himself that he is acting as a righteous man, he deprives himself of a genuine spiritual life and begins to live in prelest. He then begins to persuade everyone else of the correctness of his way. The more his conscience pricks him, the more energetically the man lunges into an active justification of his path. At this point, the enemy is glad to join in and he further inspires the man and can even energize him for this endeavor. If God does not stop the process by interceding, the man will not only destroy himself, but can often take down with him numerous souls who trust him.

"Take heed" Christ commanded us *"lest any man deceive you: For many shall come in my name, saying, I am Christ; and shall deceive many".* (Mark 13:5), (Matt: 24:4,5). The deception which is predicted in this scriptural passage by Christ, will be so widespread on earth in the last times, that Christ was even brought to ask whether He shall find faith at all upon His return (Luke 18:8).

Yet Christ *will* find that Faith, although at the end there will be very little of it. Christ did promise invincibility to His Church, for He said *"I will build my Church and the gates of hell shall not prevail against Her"* (Mat 16:18).

The purpose of every Orthodox Christian is not to "save the Church", or to "re-build" the Church. Christ Himself, who built the Church is the only Head of the Church and, according to His promise, is always taking care of His Church. He promised us "lo, I am with you always, until the end of the ages" (Mat 28:20).

The purpose of every orthodox Christian is not to "save the Church" but rather for *himself* to be saved in the Church. For only the True Faith can save a man, and the True Faith only exists completely in the true original Church, in the One, Holy, Catholic and Apostolic Church - The Holy Orthodox Church.

Christ exhorted His disciples and Apostles on the very eve of His sufferings on the Cross, saying: *"I have told you all this so you may have peace in Me. In the world you will have tribulations and sorrows. But take courage, I have overcome the world"* (John 16:33). *"Let not your heart be troubled: ye believe in God, believe also in me"* (John 14:1).

But we cannot be naïve, "For our struggle is not against flesh and blood, but against the rulers, against the authorities, against the powers of darkness of this world, against the spirits of wickedness in the aerial realm beneath the heavens" (Ephesians 6:12). (These are various ranks of evil spirits or demons). Apostle Peter warns us "Be sober, be watchful: your enemy, the devil, as a roaring lion, walketh about, seeking whom he may devour" (1 Peter 5:8). And Christ instructed His disciples, "I am sending you out like sheep among wolves. Be ye therefore wise as serpents and simple as doves" (Mat 10:16).

This Faith that Jesus Christ wants us to have and live by is the pure Apostolic Faith, the genuine patristic Faith - the holy Orthodox Faith. As was mentioned in the introduction of this book, the world has strayed far from that faith. In order to acquire that pure simple and genuine Faith in Jesus Christ our God, we must have a humble heart, a contrite spirit, a childlike purity and a flaming love for God.

Such a Faith, a True Faith, is capable of uniting all the faithful into One. The enemy of mankind, of course, does not have such a Faith, but in attempting to imitate Christ and His Church, he also summons all to join and be "one". But the unification promised by the enemy is false, based on a false faith, on prelest. Therefore, the unification of the enemy, although every attempt will be made to achieve it, will turn out to be impossible.

Genuine unification, can be granted only by God Himself to mankind. For this was God's purpose in creating man, so that men would be *one* not only with one another but even with God Himself, communing of the inexpressibly blessed Life and the Unity of the Most Holy Trinity.

After the Mystical Supper and the final parting conversation with the disciples before His Redeeming Cross, Christ prayed to God the Father: *"Neither pray I for these alone, but for them also which shall believe on me through their word; that they all may be one; as thou, Father, art in me, and I in thee, that they also may be one in us: that the world may believe that thou hast sent me."* (John 17:20,21).

Glory to Our God+